Avventura

Avventura

JOURNEYS IN ITALIAN CUISINE

with David Rocco

BAY
BOOKS
SAN FRANCISCO

Avventura is the companion volume to the Public Television series, "Avventura, Journeys in Italian Cuisine:"

a Catalyst Entertainment production in association with Rockhead Productions Inc., distributed by Gullane

Pictures LLC and Catalyst Distribution Inc., www.avventuratv.com

Bay Books is an imprint of Bay Books & Tapes, Inc.

555 De Haro St., No. 220, San Francisco, CA 94107

Publisher: James Connolly

Editorial Director: Floyd Yearout

Book Design: Design Site

Text: Sharon Silva

Food Photographer: Maren Caruso

Food Photographer's Assistant: Faiza Ali

Food Stylists: Kimberly Konecny, Erin Quon

Prop Stylist: Carol Hacker / Table Prop

Library of Congress Cataloging-in-Publication

Rocco, David.

    Avventura: journeys in Italian cuisine / David Rocco.

        p.cm.

    Includes index.

    ISBN 1-57959-510-3

1. Cookery, Italian. I. Title.

TX723 .R5346 2000

641.5945-dc21   00-023613

Printed in China

10 9 8 7 6 5 4 3 2 1

Distributed by Publishers Group West

VISIT THE WORLD'S MOST EXOTIC LOCATIONS IN SEARCH OF SAVORY INDIGENOUS CUISINE.

Come with Avventura on our Gourmet Excursion through Italy,
exploring the countryside and its food with host, David Rocco.

Inviting you on a Gourmet Excursion . . .

CONTENTS

CONTENTS

Lake Garda

t is the bluest, biggest, and arguably the most beautiful of the fabled Italian Lakes. Located in Italy's scenic northeast, with its western bank in Lombardy, its eastern shore in the Veneto, and its northern tip anchored firmly in Trentino, Lake Garda—Lago di Garda—has been a favorite destination of poets and playwrights, lovers and layabouts, the wealthy and the working class for centuries. Nicknamed the Riviera of the Dolomites, for the nearby mountains that remain snow-capped much of the year, the lake boasts a captivating Mediterranean landscape of lemon and orange groves, carefully tended vineyards, and ancient olive trees stretching away from the water's edge.

A leisurely ride on one of the steamers that circles the lake is the most scenic—and romantic—way to take in the sights. A number of towns dot the shore, many of them sporting a handsome *castello*—some intact, some crumbling. At the foot of Mount Baldo on the east coast, Malcésine, with its narrow medieval streets, is home to the thirteenth-century Scaliger Castle, which rises from a promontory that juts out into the lake, framing stunning views from its imposing tower. South of Malcésine at Bardolino, with its nineteenth-century villas and legendary vineyards, savvy connoisseurs sip the famous red wine at its source. At the southern tip of the lake, the lovely Sirmione, immortalized by the poet Catullus and site of a large Roman bath, draws visitors to its thermal spa and its small turreted harbor filled with colorful boats.

Towns and villages punctuate the shore of Lake Garda. Nearly every one of them harbors a complement of trattorias that show off the local fare of fish grilled with herbs, fresh pastas tossed with sauces built on the region's fragrant olive oil, and wild mushrooms gathered in nearby forests. Below is the fortified port in the popular resort town of Sirmione on the Southern shore of the lake.

ROLLED SALMON TROUT WITH SWEET HERBS

INVOLTINI DI TROTA GRATINATA

SERVES FOUR

Salmon trout flourish in Lake Garda, and the region's fishermen keep local cooks happy by supplying their town markets with the prized fish. This simple main course, which can be assembled a few hours in advance and refrigerated until baking, shows off this coveted catch at its best.

Preparation:

1 Preheat the oven to 375°F.

2 In a bowl, combine the tomatoes with the basil, 2 tablespoons olive oil, and salt to taste, crushing the tomatoes to make a "fresh" tomato sauce. Set aside.

3 Slice the trout fillets on the bias to make 12 thin slices of approximately 2 ounces each. Spread $1/2$ cup of the crumb mixture on a work surface. Lay the trout slices on the bread crumbs to coat the underside. Season the tops of the slices with salt and sprinkle with the chives. Sprinkle the remaining 1 cup crumb mixture over the slices, then roll into cylinders.

4 Pour half of the flavored olive oil into a shallow baking dish just large enough to accommodate the salmon rolls in a single layer without touching. Place the rolls, seam side down, in the dish. Drizzle the remaining flavored olive oil over the top. Then spoon the tomato sauce evenly over the rolls.

5 Place in the oven and bake until the fish is just opaque at the center when tested with a knife, 6 to 8 minutes. Remove from the oven and serve immediately on warmed plates.

$1 1/2$ CUPS DRAINED CANNED PLUM TOMATOES, PREFERABLY SAN MARZANO VARIETY

1 TABLESPOON CHOPPED FRESH BASIL

2 TABLESPOONS EXTRA-VIRGIN OLIVE OIL

SALT

$1 1/2$ POUNDS SALMON TROUT FILLETS

$1 1/2$ CUPS FINE DRIED BREAD CRUMBS SEASONED WITH 2 TABLESPOONS EACH MINCED FRESH BASIL, THYME, ROSEMARY, AND CHIVES

ABOUT 2 TABLESPOONS MINCED FRESH CHIVES

$1/2$ CUP EXTRA-VIRGIN OLIVE OIL FLAVORED WITH 1 TABLESPOON EACH MINCED FRESH BASIL AND ROSEMARY; 2 CLOVES GARLIC, CRUSHED; AND SALT TO TASTE

SQUID STUFFED WITH SALMON
CALAMARI RIPIENI CON SALMONE

SERVES FOUR

Lake Garda draws visitors from all walks of life, from the elite of Milan who occupy the five-star hotels to day-trippers from Verona who arrive by bus. All of them enjoy good food, however, such as this lovely antipasto served at the Gardesana restaurant, located in the small scenic town of Torri del Benaco, on the southeast shore of the lake. When the weather is fair, diners enjoy eating on the patio, with its splendid views of the lake.

4 LARGE SQUID, EACH 6 TO 8 INCHES LONG

1/4 POUND FRESH SALMON FILLET, CHOPPED

1/4 POUND SMOKED SALMON, CHOPPED

1 EGG

1 TABLESPOON BRANDY

1 TABLESPOON CHOPPED FRESH CHIVES

SALT AND FRESHLY GROUND BLACK PEPPER

4 CUPS MIXED YOUNG SALAD GREENS

EXTRA-VIRGIN OLIVE OIL FOR DRIZZLING

JUICE OF 2 LEMONS

Preparation:

1 First, clean the squid: Working with 1 squid at a time, cut off the tentacles just above the eyes. Squeeze the base of the tentacles to pop out the hard beak. Rinse the tentacles well and set aside whole. Pull out and discard the cartilage-like "quill" from the body, then rinse the body well, discarding the entrails. Carefully pull off the thin, mottled skin that covers the body, rinse the body again, and set aside. Repeat with the remaining squid and pat dry.

2 In a blender, combine the fresh salmon, smoked salmon, egg, brandy, chives, and salt and pepper to taste, and purée until creamy.

3 Spoon the salmon puree into a pastry bag and, working with 1 squid body at a time, pipe the purée into the body. Bring the top edges of the body together to enclose the filling, tucking the base of the tentacles into the opening. Secure the top closed and the tentacles in place with a toothpick.

4 Bring a wide saucepan three-fourths full of water to a boil. Carefully slip the stuffed squid into the pan, adjust the heat to keep the water at a gentle boil, and cook uncovered, until opaque, 10 to 15 minutes. Using a slotted utensil, transfer the squid to a plate, let cool, then cover and refrigerate until well chilled, about 2 hours.

5 Remove the squid from the refrigerator, discard the toothpicks, and thinly slice the squid crosswise. Arrange the greens on a platter and top with the sliced squid. Drizzle with olive oil and lemon juice and sprinkle with salt to taste. Serve at once.

Stresa

I n the nineteenth century, well-to-do British regularly set out on a Grand Tour of the Continent. In Italy, they would inevitably stop at the holiday resort town of Stresa, to take in the views of Lake Maggiore and the Swiss Alps, all the while relishing the pleasant climate—a climate their own country denied them. In the following century, Ernest Hemingway stayed in Stresa, was charmed by it, and decided to make the aristocratic Grand Hotel des Iles Borromées, with its Belle Époque furnishings and flower-carpeted gardens, a location in his estimable *A Farewell to Arms*. But long before any of these fussy travelers dis-covered Stresa and the lake, the Italian nobility were bewitched by the region. During the Renaissance, they built dozens of elegant villas and castles here, many of which can be visited today.

Lake Maggiore, which rambles for more than forty miles between Piedmont and Lombardy and is lined with seasonal flowers—camellia, verbena, azalea—ends just across the border in Switzerland. Sojourners with a short time here typically decide to concentrate on Stresa, with its countless *gelato* stands, fine boutiques, excellent restaurants, and tiny, climbing streets, and on the small, strikingly picturesque Borromean Islands in the azure waters just beyond the town. The islands are named for the Borromeo family of Milan, who over the centuries dotted them with family *palazzi*. Indeed, the beautiful—and appropriately named—Isola Bella has been part of the Milanese dynasty's real estate holdings since the twelfth century.

Its history of wealthy residents has made Stresa rich in statuary and fountains, well-tended gardens, and grand villas. The dinner table is opulent, drawing on what is cultivated, caught, or made in the region: from corn, rice, and wheat to chestnuts, hazelnuts, and walnuts to tench, pike, and whitefish to chocolate, cheeses, and *grissini*. And, of course, a *buca* of Piedmontese wines—Barolo, Barbera, Moscato—makes every local meal a feast.

POLENTA WITH SEASONED BEEF
POLENTA CON TAPULONE DI MANZO

SERVES FOUR

Although instant polenta is available, the best polenta is made from regular grain and stirred slowly and steadily over medium heat for one half hour. If you have some polenta left over, shape it into a flat, thin sheet, allow it to cool and become solid, and then cut it into squares or other shapes, and fry or grill as an accompaniment to meat, fish, or vegetable dishes.

FOR THE BEEF:

1 TABLESPOON UNSALTED BUTTER

1 TABLESPOON LARD OR RENDERED BACON FAT

2 TABLESPOONS EXTRA-VIRGIN OLIVE OIL

2 SMALL YELLOW ONIONS, FINELY CHOPPED

3 CLOVES GARLIC, FINELY CHOPPED

1 CUP FINELY SHREDDED SAVOY CABBAGE

1 1/4 POUNDS LEAN GROUND BEEF

3 WHOLE CLOVES

1 1/2 TEASPOONS FENNEL SEEDS

2 BAY LEAVES

SALT AND FRESHLY GROUND BLACK PEPPER

1/2 CUP FULL-BODIED DRY RED WINE SUCH AS BARBERA

1 TO 2 CUPS BEEF STOCK (PAGE 159) OR VEGETABLE STOCK (PAGE 158), OR AS NEEDED

FOR THE POLENTA:

10 CUPS (2 1/2 QUARTS) WATER

1 1/2 TEASPOONS SEA SALT

2 CUPS POLENTA

2 TABLESPOONS UNSALTED BUTTER

Preparation:

1 First, prepare the beef: In a large frying pan over medium heat, melt the butter and lard (or bacon fat) with the olive oil. Add the onions and garlic and sauté until they soften, 2 to 3 minutes. Add the cabbage and cook, stirring, until it wilts, about 2 minutes. Add the beef, cloves, fennel seeds, bay leaves, and salt and pepper to taste and mix thoroughly. Continue to cook, stirring frequently and breaking up the beef as necessary, until the meat is evenly browned, about 5 minutes.

2 Raise the heat to medium-high, pour in the wine, and cook, stirring often, until almost all the liquid has evaporated, about 5 minutes. Ladle in 1 cup of the stock, reduce the heat to medium-low, and simmer gently uncovered, stirring occasionally, until the flavors are well blended and most of the liquid has evaporated, about 30 minutes. Add more stock during cooking if the mixture begins to dry out. When ready, it should have a rich, saucy consistency.

3 While the beef is cooking, prepare the polenta: Pour the water into a large saucepan, add the salt, and bring to a boil over high heat. Add the polenta in a thin, steady stream while stirring continuously to prevent the formation of lumps. Reduce the heat to medium and continue to cook, stirring constantly, until the polenta pulls away from the sides of the pan and no longer has a gritty taste, 30 to 40 minutes. Stir in the butter (this will create a creamy consistency) and adjust the seasoning with salt.

4 To serve, divide the polenta among warmed plates and spoon the beef over the top. Serve immediately.

Valle d'Aosta

The smallest of Italy's twenty regions, Valle d'Aosta delivers towering peaks, emerald valleys, leafy chestnut groves, and vineyards heavy with wine grapes. The residents, who seem to thrive in the mild alpine climate, look out on the Continent's highest mountains—Mont Blanc, the Matterhorn, Monte Rosa, Gran Paradiso—pull fish from crystal clear lakes and streams, protect a wealth of Roman ruins and Romanesque churches, live in slate-roofed stone cottages, and welcome visitors to a cluster of first-class winter and summer resorts.

Once the private hunting grounds of the Italian royal family, today much of Valle d'Aosta is part of the Gran Paradiso National Park, which it shares with neighboring Piedmont. In spring, the meadows are a sea of wildflowers and herbs, which draw the chamois, ibex, and wild goats down from the mountaintops to feed, and give the local honey, called *millefiori* (a thousand flowers), its distinctive flavor. Cows, which outnumber humans in the region, graze on the high pastures, too, and their milk is turned into Fontina cheese, a wonderfully nutty, rich *formaggio* that has been made in these highlands for more than seven centuries.

Cogne stands at the center of the park. In the winter months, its hotels and hostels are filled with alpine and cross-country skiers, while in the summertime, hikers occupy the same spaces. Come evening, tired from the day's activities, these outdoor enthusiasts take in the local culinary specialties, such as *prosciutto* cured with alpine herbs and *polenta concia*, cooked with Fontina and butter.

Frescoed churches, imposing fortresses, crenellated turrets, and Roman bridges all reflect Valle d'Aosta's long, colorful history. In the kitchen, that same history has conspired with a dramatic landscape to create a rustic table that draws upon such regional ingredients as beef and game, butter and handmade cheeses, hearty dark rye breads, air-cured sausages, chestnuts, wild berries, honey, and straw-colored *renetta* apples. Génépy, the potent local grappa, is infused with the flowers of mountain herbs.

RISOTTO WITH FONTINA AND CROSTINI
RISOTTO CON FONTINA E CROSTINI

SERVES 4

The buttery Fontina cheese produced in Valle d'Aosta is legendary, and this simple risotto showcases it beautifully. For a more elaborate dish, simply increase the ingredients to create one or two additional layers of rice, *crostini*, and cheese. Top only the final layer with cinnamon and melted butter. A whole-wheat country bread is typically used for the *crostini*, but a crusty white loaf also works well.

FOR THE *CROSTINI*:

2 TABLESPOONS UNSALTED BUTTER

6 THIN SLICES CRUSTY BREAD, CUT ON THE DIAGONAL FROM A LONG, SLENDER LOAF

FOR THE RISOTTO:

6 CUPS BEEF STOCK (PAGE 159)

½ CUP UNSALTED BUTTER

½ CUP FINELY CHOPPED YELLOW ONION

2 CUPS ARBORIO RICE

½ CUP DRY WHITE WINE

4 TO 6 SLICES FONTINA CHEESE (ABOUT 1 OUNCE EACH)

GROUND CINNAMON FOR SPRINKLING

Preparation:

1 To make the *crostini*, in a large frying pan, melt the butter over medium heat. Add the bread slices and sauté, turning as needed, until golden brown on both sides, about 5 minutes total. Transfer to a plate and set aside.

2 Preheat the oven to 375°F.

3 To make the risotto, pour the stock into a saucepan, bring to a simmer, then adjust the heat to keep the liquid hot. In a heavy saucepan over medium-low heat, melt ¼ cup of the butter. Add the onion and sauté until translucent, about 5 minutes. Add the rice and stir until the grains are well coated and opaque, about 2 minutes. Add the wine and stir until reduced by half. Then add a ladleful (about ¾ cup) of the stock, adjust the heat to maintain a gentle simmer, and cook, stirring continuously, until the stock is absorbed. Continue adding the stock, a ladleful at a time and stirring continuously, until the rice is just tender but still slightly firm in the center. The total cooking time should be about 18 minutes, at which point the risotto should be moist and creamy. Remember to add more hot stock only after each ladleful is absorbed. Remove from the heat.

4 Spoon the risotto into a deep baking dish and arrange the crostini on top in a single layer. They should cover the surface completely. Lay the cheese slices on the *crostini*, again making sure they cover the surface completely. Sprinkle evenly with a light dusting of cinnamon, then melt the remaining ¼ cup butter and drizzle evenly over the top.

5 Place the baking dish in the oven for about 5 minutes to melt the cheese slightly. Serve hot directly from the dish.

La Spezia

The province of La Spezia, in Italy's northwest region of Liguria, lays claim to some of the most memorable seafront expanses in Italy. Along this scenic stretch, part of the so-called Italian Riviera, coves and cliffs shelter well-worn villages of ochre and pastel houses backed by olive trees, sage, and myrtle and fronted by sandy strands. The busy town of La Spezia, its modern face the result of Allied bombing, stands at the head of a graceful bay, making it a practical jumping-off point for some the region's best-known attractions.

The fabled Cinque Terre, five small towns—Monterosso, Vernazza, Corniglia, Manarola, Riomaggiore—perched amid jagged cliffs or climbing away from pebbly beaches, lie just north of La Spezia. Precipitous footpaths with stunning views at every turn connect the picture-postcard communities. Near the towns, vineyards march along narrow terraces, with much of their harvest turned into the region's straw-colored wines. At the little known, tiny Manarola, a small fishing fleet bobs in the harbor, while its captains mend nets in the warm afternoon sun.

South of La Spezia is Lerici, which proved a magnet for British writers in the nineteenth and early twentieth centuries. D. H. Lawrence and Lord Byron lived here for a time, and Percy and Mary Shelley settled in a villa, the Casa Magni, in the nearby village of San Terenzo. The inspiration for Mary Shelley's classic novel, *Frankenstein*, was the local imposing—and appropriately scary—castle, visible from her balcony.

La Spezia has long been home to seafarers, and grilled and fried fish are central to the province's cuisine. Vegetables are stuffed with all manner of ingredients, focaccia is brushed with olive oil and flavored with rosemary, and chickpea flour is baked into large disks that are cut and sold as traveling sustenance. Grapes from vineyards high above the sea go into the making of Sciacchetrà, a notable dessert wine the color of amber.

MIXED FRIED FISH
FRITTURA DI BARCA

Italy's long coastline makes a simple *frittura di barca*—fish fry from the boat—a popular dish at the country's many seaside resorts. Other small fish that may be more readily available, such as whitebait, small mullets, and sardines, can be used. This amount will serve four as a first course, but it can be easily increased and offered as a main.

Preparation:

1 Clean all the fish, rinse well, and pat dry with paper towels. Sprinkle the fish on both sides with salt, then dust with flour, coating evenly and shaking off any excess.

2 Pour the oil to a depth of about 3 inches into a deep fryer or deep, heavy saucepan and heat to 375°F. When the oil is hot, add the fish, in batches, and fry, turning as necessary, until golden brown, 2 to 3 minutes. Using a wire skimmer, transfer to paper towels to drain briefly.

3 Arrange the fish on a warmed serving platter with the lemon quarters and serve immediately.

$\frac{1}{3}$ POUND BABY SOLE

$\frac{1}{3}$ POUND BABY EELS

$\frac{1}{3}$ POUND FRESH ANCHOVIES

$\frac{1}{3}$ POUND SMELTS

SALT

ALL-PURPOSE FLOUR FOR DUSTING

OLIVE OIL FOR DEEP-FRYING

1 LEMON, QUARTERED

ANCHOVIES CURED IN WHITE WINE VINEGAR

ACCIUGHE AL'AGRO

SERVES 4

Italian cooks sometimes cover fresh anchovies with seasoned bread crumbs and bake them, or they coat them with egg and bread crumbs and fry them in olive oil. Here, the fresh fish are simply cured in wine vinegar and then topped with tomatoes, onions, basil, and a thread of olive oil. You can increase all the ingredients in this recipe and make two or three layers of the dressed anchovies.

12 FRESH ANCHOVIES

2 LEMONS, HALVED

6 TO 8 TABLESPOONS WHITE WINE VINEGAR

SALT AND FRESHLY GROUND BLACK PEPPER

4 RIPE TOMATOES, CHOPPED

1 SMALL YELLOW ONION, FINELY CHOPPED

6 TO 8 FRESH BASIL LEAVES

EXTRA-VIRGIN OLIVE OIL FOR DRIZZLING

Preparation:

1 To clean the anchovies, work with 1 fish at a time: Pull off the head, which will split open the body cavity, and remove the innards. Run your finger down the middle of the opened fish, lifting up and discarding the backbone and the tail. Rinse the fish under cold running water, drain well, and pat dry. Repeat with the remaining anchovies.

2 Arrange the cleaned anchovies, skin side down, in a single layer on a shallow nonreactive dish. Squeeze the juice from the lemon halves over them, then pour on the vinegar and season with salt. Cover and place in the refrigerator for 2 to 3 hours to allow the anchovies to cure. They are ready when they have become opaque.

3 Pour off the vinegar and lemon juice, and season the anchovies with salt and pepper. Sprinkle the tomatoes and onion over the fish. Then tear the basil leaves into pieces and strew the pieces over the anchovies. Drizzle with olive oil and add a little more pepper, if desired. Serve at room temperature.

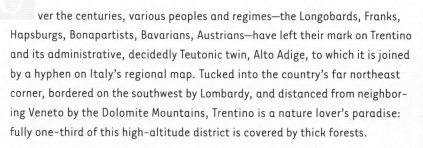

Trentino

ver the centuries, various peoples and regimes—the Longobards, Franks, Hapsburgs, Bonapartists, Bavarians, Austrians—have left their mark on Trentino and its administrative, decidedly Teutonic twin, Alto Adige, to which it is joined by a hyphen on Italy's regional map. Tucked into the country's far northeast corner, bordered on the southwest by Lombardy, and distanced from neighboring Veneto by the Dolomite Mountains, Trentino is a nature lover's paradise: fully one-third of this high-altitude district is covered by thick forests.

Below the mountaintops lies the ancient and sophisticated regional capital of Trento, a favorite spot from which to explore the alpine surroundings and set out for the many local ski resorts. Nestled in a green bowl, the city is the site of an old Roman forum and of a statuesque Romanesque *duomo*, begun in the thirteenth century and finished some three hundred years later. Across from the *duomo*, the via Belenzani leads north, with Venetian-style houses marching along it.

The Castello del Buon Consiglio, now a national museum, is here too. And it is not alone. Trentino is said to have some 150 castles—more than any other region in Italy—and, of course, each has its own story. Locals love to relate tales of advancing armies fought off from the towers of the fortified *castelli*, and of the ghosts who now roam their halls. The legends are inevitably told over glasses of locally made grappa, for tiny Trentino produces some 10 percent of all such spirits bottled in the country.

This mountainous region, with its green valleys, trout-filled rivers, *piazza*-laced towns, and modern ski resorts, enjoys a hearty Italian table marked by an Austrian accent: *pasta e fagioli* soup, sausages with sauerkraut, *bollito misto*. Polenta, mushrooms, chestnuts, and locally made cow's milk cheeses are pantry staples, and the harvest from the region's many apple orchards is used in everything from risotto, fritters, and strudel to a fine *acquavita*.

PORK SPARERIBS WITH DARK POLENTA AND MUSHROOMS
PUNTINE DI MALALE CON POLENTA MORA

SERVES FOUR

In Trentino, cooks use porcini and small wild mushrooms gathered locally, called *finferli*, for this dish. But cultivated white mushrooms make an acceptable substitute, preferably mixed with porcini or the more easily obtainable portobellos. The reference to "dark polenta" comes from using buckwheat polenta along with the more common corn polenta. Guests will be surprised to see the usual yellow mound replaced by one with an earthier color. If you cannot find the buckwheat product, increase the corn polenta to 2 cups.

Preparation:

1 Prepare a fire in a charcoal grill.

2 To prepare the spareribs, season them on both sides of the slabs with salt and pepper to taste, then sprinkle both sides with garlic powder, rosemary, thyme, and tarragon. Smear the mustard on both sides of the slabs, covering the surface completely. Rub the mustard well into the meat.

3 When the coals are ready, place the spareribs, bone side down (the side with the least meat exposed), on the grill rack 8 to 10 inches above the fire. Cook for about 1 hour, then turn and cook the meat until nicely browned, about 30 minutes longer. The pork is done when it has pulled away about 1/4 inch from the ends of the bones.

4 About 45 minutes before the spareribs are ready, begin preparing the polenta: Pour the water into a large saucepan, add salt to taste, and bring to a boil over high heat. Combine the polentas and add them in a thin, steady stream while stirring continuously to prevent the formation of lumps. Add the olive oil (this will result in a smoother texture and will also perfume the polenta), reduce the heat to medium, and continue to cook, stirring constantly, until the polenta pulls away from the sides of the pan and no longer has a gritty taste, 30 to 40 minutes. Remove from the heat and keep warm.

CONTINUED ON THE NEXT PAGE

FOR THE SPARERIBS:

4 1/2 POUNDS PORK SPARERIBS, IN SLABS

SALT AND FRESHLY GROUND BLACK PEPPER

2 TABLESPOONS GARLIC POWDER

1 TABLESPOON DRIED ROSEMARY

1 TABLESPOON DRIED THYME

1 TABLESPOON DRIED TARRAGON

3/4 CUP DIJON MUSTARD

FOR THE POLENTA:

10 CUPS (2 1/2 QUARTS) WATER

SALT

1 1/2 CUPS CORN POLENTA

1/2 CUP SARACEN (BUCKWHEAT) POLENTA

1 1/2 TABLESPOONS EXTRA-VIRGIN OLIVE OIL

PORK SPARERIBS WITH DARK POLENTA AND MUSHROOMS

PUNTINE DI MAIALE CON POLENTA MORA

FOR THE MUSHROOMS:

1 ½ TEASPOONS EXTRA-VIRGIN OLIVE OIL

2 CUPS SLICED MIXED FRESH PORCINI AND CULTIVATED WHITE MUSHROOMS

2 CLOVES GARLIC, CHOPPED

½ CUP DRY WHITE WINE

½ CUP HEAVY CREAM

2 TABLESPOONS CHOPPED FRESH FLAT-LEAF PARSLEY

SALT

CONTINUED FROM THE PREVIOUS PAGE

5 To prepare the mushrooms, in a large frying pan over medium-high heat, warm the olive oil. When the oil is hot, add the mushrooms and garlic and sauté until the mushrooms release their liquid, 2 to 3 minutes. Add the wine and continue to cook until it evaporates. Then pour in the cream and simmer until the cream reduces to a fairly thick mixture, 2 to 3 minutes. Stir in the parsley and season to taste with salt. Remove from the heat.

6 To serve, cut the ribs apart and arrange an equal number of the ribs on each warmed plate. Place a good-sized mound of polenta alongside and top with the mushrooms. Serve at once.

Florence

Florence

t is a jewel, a place that balances a rich past with a lively present. From the *duomo* to the Ponte Vecchio, from Santa Croce to the Uffizi, Florence—*Firenze* in Italian—is a showcase of Italian art, history, culture, and style. Hugging the shores of the Arno River, this fabled city of north-central Tuscany reveals its undeniable glory in a nearly continuous string of Gothic, Romanesque, and especially Renaissance buildings, and seals its place in history books with such names as Medici, Michelangelo, and Machiavelli.

Visitors to the city are automatically drawn to the extensive art collections, delicate loggias, and fading frescoes. Yet they are also attracted by the daily life of the Florentines, many of whom buy clothes from the street vendors at bustling San Lorenzo market and "treasures" from persuasive merchants at the flea market in Piazza dei Ciompi. The more monied locals shop at the old-line auction houses and seek out their linens and woolens at long-established fabric stores. But everyone heads to the Mercato Centrale for food, pausing at stalls offering goods fresh from the surrounding countryside.

Then, come early evening, the Florentines—and their visitors—set out on their *passeggiata*, walking with family and friends through the streets, perhaps stopping for a *gelato* at Vivoli or Perché No?, Florence's two most popular ice cream shops. It is, alas, a smug crowd, for these strollers know that they are at home in what many travelers consider Italy's most captivating city.

Although Florence is undeniably rich in art treasures, its *cucina* is one of delicious restraint. Florentine cooks rely on high-quality raw materials, a minimum of sauces, and local olive oil to produce such signature dishes as *bistecca alla fiorentina*, ravioli filled with spinach and ricotta, and *pollo alla diavola* (grilled chicken flattened with a brick). And who can resist dunking *biscotti di Prato* into a glass of *vin santo*, Tuscany's legendary sweet wine?

COUSCOUS SALAD AND PORCINI "IN A BAG"
COUSCOUS IN PANZANELLA E PORCINI IN CARTOCCIO

The couscous is prepared much like *panzanella*, a famed Tuscan peasant salad in which day-old bread is soaked in olive oil, vinegar, and other ingredients. The mushrooms are cooked *in cartoccio*, "in a bag." Here the bag is an aluminum foil boat set afloat in a *bagno maria* to cook. You may substitute porcini mushrooms with fresh portobellos. In Tuscany, a mint—like herb known as *nepitella* (calamint in English) is used, but any common mint can be substituted. Include plenty of good coarse country bread at the table for guests to sop up the delicious juices from the mushrooms.

FOR THE COUSCOUS:

1 CUP CANNED PLUM TOMATOES WITH THEIR JUICES, PREFERABLY SAN MARZANO VARIETY

1/2 CUP EXTRA-VIRGIN OLIVE OIL

1/2 CUP FRESH LEMON JUICE

1 1/2 CUPS INSTANT COUSCOUS

1/2 CUP CHOPPED YELLOW BELL PEPPER

1/2 CUP FINELY CHOPPED YELLOW ONION

1/2 CUP FINELY CHOPPED CUCUMBER

1/2 CUP HALVED CHERRY TOMATOES

1/2 CUP CHOPPED CELERY

1/4 CUP CHOPPED FRESH BASIL

1/4 CUP CHOPPED FRESH FLAT-LEAF PARSLEY

1 TABLESPOON DRIED OREGANO

SALT, FRESHLY GROUND BLACK PEPPER, AND RED PEPPER FLAKES

FOR THE MUSHROOMS:

8 FRESH PORCINI, STEMMED AND BRUSHED CLEAN

4 CLOVES GARLIC, FINELY SLIVERED

3/4 CUP EXTRA-VIRGIN OLIVE OIL

CHOPPED FRESH OREGANO AND MINT FOR SPRINKLING

SALT AND FRESHLY GROUND BLACK PEPPER

Preparation:

1 To prepare the couscous, place the tomatoes and their juices in a large bowl and crush them completely. Add the olive oil, lemon juice, and uncooked couscous and mix well. Then add all the remaining ingredients, including salt, black pepper, and red pepper flakes to taste. Cover and refrigerate for at least 1 hour to allow the liquid and the juices from the vegetables to plump the couscous. The salad will be even tastier if allowed to mellow for up to 4 hours or so.

2 To prepare the mushrooms, preheat the oven to 350°F. Cut 2 pieces of aluminum foil each about 12 inches long. They must be large enough to accommodate 2 mushrooms placed side by side, with plenty of overhang for enclosing the mushrooms and sealing the packet securely. Stack the 2 sheets and place 2 mushroom caps in the center. Pierce each cap several times with a small paring knife, and insert 3 or 4 pieces of garlic in each cap. Drizzle 3 tablespoons of the olive oil over the mushrooms and sprinkle with the oregano, mint, salt, and pepper to taste. Lift up the corners of the aluminum foil to meet, fold over the edges, and seal tightly. The package should be airtight. Repeat with the remaining mushrooms, forming 4 packets in all.

3 Select a shallow roasting pan and pour in boiling water to a depth of 1 1/2 inches. Place the packets in the water—they will float like little boats. Slip the pan into the oven and bake until the mushrooms are tender and fragrant, 15 to 20 minutes. To test for doneness, open a packet seal and pierce the mushrooms with a knife.

4 To serve, distribute the packets among individual plates and let each diner open his or her own packet, releasing the exquisite aroma. Serve the salad alongside the packet or pass it at the table in an attractive serving bowl.

Visitors to the spa towns of the Euganean Hills are greeted by grand tree-lined promenades outfitted with elegant fountains.

Terme Euganee

I n the Veneto, tucked between the Euganean Hills and the ancient city of Padua, are the Euganean thermal spas—Terme Euganee in Italian—known as Ábano Terme and Montegrotto Terme. For much of the year, they are packed with people in search of the legendary health cures and beauty treatments delivered by the water that races down from high in the Dolomites, gathering therapeutic minerals along the way. At the end of the journey, the water, now bubbling thermal springs, becomes a series of bathing pools or is mixed with the local clay for a hot mud bath guaranteed to ease rheumatism and to give tired skin new luster.

Most visitors who "take the waters" also take time to visit the nearby medieval village of Arquà Petrarca, which stands near the southern edge of the Euganean Hills. It is named for Francesco Petrarca (Petrarch), the creator of the sonnet form. He spent his last years here, dying in 1374—his red marble tomb stands in front of the church of Santa Maria—and over the centuries his home has been an important pilgrimage site, welcoming such visitors as Mozart, Shelley, and Byron.

Hundreds of sixteenth-century villas, some of them the work of Padua-born architect Andrea di Pietro della Gondola, better known as Palladio, rise in the surrounding countryside, and they, too, make interesting side trips after a day at a spa. These imposing structures were the property of Venetians, who, wealthy from shipping, turned to agriculture and built summer homes from which to administer their vast estates.

COLD ORECCHIETTE WITH TUNA
ORECCHIETTE FREDDE

In the heat of the Veneto summer, this cold pasta dish is a refreshing main course. It can be prepared early in the morning, and then served when the sun has made the day too hot to cook. If you cannot find stracciatella cheese, a fresh cow's milk cheese popular in the region, fresh mozzarella, preferably made from water buffalo's milk, may be substituted.

SALT

1 POUND FRESH OR DRIED *ORECCHIETTE*

EXTRA-VIRGIN OLIVE OIL, AS NEEDED

1 POUND FRESH TUNA FILLET, FINELY DICED

FRESHLY GRATED LEMON ZEST

3 TABLESPOONS FRESH LEMON JUICE

5 TABLESPOONS DRY WHITE WINE

5 TABLESPOONS MILK

2 EGGS

2 TEASPOONS UNSALTED BUTTER

1 POUND CHERRY TOMATOES, STEMMED AND CHOPPED

1 BUNCH ARUGULA, STEMMED AND CHOPPED

2 TABLESPOONS GRATED PARMIGIANO-REGGIANO CHEESE

5 TABLESPOONS FINELY DICED STRACCIATELLA CHEESE

Preparation:

1 Bring a large saucepan filled with water to a boil. Add salt to taste and the pasta, stir well, and cook until *al dente*, about 3 minutes for fresh pasta or 10 minutes for dried pasta, or according to package instructions. Drain well, place under cold running water to cool, transfer to a bowl, and toss with about 1 tablespoon olive oil to prevent the pasta from sticking together.

2 In a frying pan over medium heat, warm about 1 tablespoon olive oil. Add the tuna and fry, stirring occasionally, until seared, about 1 minute. Add a dash of salt, a little grated lemon zest to taste, and the lemon juice and stir well. Add the white wine and cook, stirring occasionally, until it has evaporated, 2 to 3 minutes. Add the milk and cook, stirring occasionally, until it has evaporated, 2 to 3 minutes longer. Remove from the heat and set aside.

3 In a bowl, beat the eggs until blended. Season with salt. In another frying pan over medium heat, melt 1 teaspoon of the butter. Pour in half of the beaten egg, to form a thin sheet. (This is a simple frittata.) Cook until set and golden on the first side, then flip and cook on the second side briefly. Slip the frittata onto a cutting board. Repeat with the remaining butter and egg. Cut both frittatas into julienne strips.

4 In a large serving bowl, combine the pasta, tuna, egg strips, tomatoes, arugula, and both cheeses and toss to mix. Drizzle in olive oil, adding enough to coat all the ingredients lightly, and toss again. Season with salt, mix once again, and serve.

CHEESE WITH HONEY

SERVES FOUR

Taleggio, a smooth cow's milk cheese, is produced in Veneto, Lombardy, and Piedmont. It is typically aged about a month and a half and has a mild flavor and supple texture. Sometimes it is aged longer, becoming more aromatic and turning from white to yellow. Other cheeses, such as a pecorino sardo or pecorino romano, may be used in its place in this simple dessert.

Preparation:

1 Arrange 2 squares of cheese on each dessert plate.

2 Drizzle with honey and sprinkle with hazelnuts. Serve at once.

8 BITE-SIZED SQUARES TALEGGIO CHEESE

HONEY FOR DRIZZLING

CHOPPED HAZELNUTS FOR SPRINKLING

Genoa

he Ligurian coast is a rugged stretch that runs from Italy's border with France to Tuscany. Just beyond the midpoint of the picturesque shoreline stands Genoa—*Genova* in Italian—the country's largest port and, along with Pisa, Amalfi, and Venice, one of its ancient maritime republics. By the thirteenth century, the city, built on hills rising precipitously from the water, had set up commercial colonies from Spain to Syria to the Black Sea. It was a powerhouse, a city of bankers and businessmen, pirates and pickpockets.

Within a few centuries, Genoa had lost its overseas possessions, and today the city intrigues visitors with the landmarks that remain from its heyday. The ancient quarter is a rabbit warren of dark—some would say sinister—alleyways with almost cavelike residences. In contrast, the elegant via Garibaldi shows off a steady line of luxurious sixteenth- and seventeenth-century palaces, now used as municipal offices and other institutional headquarters.

The city has an old-fashioned character: laundry hangs to dry from windows; street-corner niches hold statues known as *madonnettes*, "little madonnas"; and *friggitorie*, local fast-food shops, sell *farinata* (thin, crisp savory cakes made from chickpea flour), fried calamari, and puffy focaccia to a steady walk-up clientele. Churches seem to be everywhere, and in fact they are. The city claims four hundred or so, many sheltering important works of art.

Genoa is home to a hardworking, food-savvy population who sit down each evening to such local specialties as *cima alla genovese* (stuffed veal breast), *pasta al pesto*, *buridda* (fish stew), and *triglie alla genovese* (mullet in a white wine and fennel sauce). Many of the ingredients for these regional plates are purchased at the city's lively Mercato Orientale, a swirl of colorful vendors, appealing products, and astute shoppers.

MIXED SEAFOOD ANTIPASTO WITH ANCHOVY CROSTINI

ANTIPASTO DI MARE CON CROSTINI

SERVES FOUR

Most restaurants in Genoa offer an antipasto that draws on the wealth of the sea, with the assortment determined by what the local fishermen have delivered to the market that morning.

Preparation:

1 Octopus is typically sold precleaned. If it has not been cleaned, invert it—much like you might turn a sock inside out—and remove the beak and viscera from the mouth, including the ink sac, rinsing well under running cold water. To tenderize it, bring a large pot of water to a boil and, holding the octopus by its mantle, dip it into the boiling water for about 10 seconds and pull it out. Let it cool slightly, then dip it again. Repeat 1 or 2 more times, then set aside.

2 Now, clean the squid and cuttlefish, using essentially the same method for both. Working with one at a time, cut off the tentacles just above the eyes. Squeeze the base of the tentacles to pop out the hard beak. Rinse the tentacles well and set aside whole. Pull out and discard the cartilage-like "quill" from the body, then rinse the body well, discarding the entrails. Carefully pull off the thin, mottled skin that covers the body, rinse the body again, and set aside with the tentacles. Repeat with the remaining squid and cuttlefish. Set aside. Rinse the shrimp and set aside.

3 In a large pot, combine the water, sea salt, onion, carrot, celery, and parsley sprigs. Cut 2 of the lemons in half, add to the pot, and bring to a boil. Add all the seafood to the pot. Remove the squid, cuttlefish, and shrimp with a slotted spoon as soon as they are cooked, after 4 to 5 minutes. Set aside to cool. Continue cooking the octopus until tender, 45 minutes to 1 1/2 hours. Transfer the octopus to a large platter and let cool. Discard the contents of the pot.

4 Peel the shrimp and leave whole. Cut the squid into rings, and cut the cuttlefish and the tentacles of the octopus into bite-sized pieces. Place all of the seafood in a large serving bowl. Cut the remaining lemon in half and squeeze the juice into the bowl. Drizzle the seafood with olive oil and add a sprinkling of chopped parsley. Season with salt and toss well. Taste and add more oil, lemon juice, parsley, and salt as needed.

5 To prepare the *crostini*, spread each bread slice with butter, then top with an anchovy fillet. Serve the seafood with the *crostini* on the side.

FOR THE SEAFOOD:

1 SMALL OCTOPUS (ABOUT 14 OUNCES)

14 OUNCES SQUID

14 OUNCES CUTTLEFISH

14 OUNCES SHRIMP IN THE SHELL

4 QUARTS WATER

1 TABLESPOON COARSE SEA SALT

1 YELLOW ONION, HALVED

1 LARGE CARROT, HALVED

2 CELERY STALKS, HALVED

3 OR 4 FRESH FLAT-LEAF PARSLEY SPRIGS, PLUS CHOPPED FRESH PARSLEY TO TASTE

3 LEMONS

EXTRA-VIRGIN OLIVE OIL

SALT

FOR THE *CROSTINI*:

8 THIN SLICES CRUSTY BREAD, CUT ON THE DIAGONAL FROM A LONG, SLENDER LOAF

UNSALTED BUTTER FOR SPREADING

8 ANCHOVY FILLETS

LINGUINE WITH PESTO

Traditional Italian cooks insist that pesto be made by hand, in a mortar, preferably of marble or ceramic. A hand-pounded sauce is said to have better color, texture, and flavor than one whirred together in a food processor or blender, although most American cooks, as well as Italians short on time, will turn to the speed and ease of a kitchen appliance.

FOR THE PESTO:

50 GOOD-SIZED FRESH BASIL LEAVES
(1 1/2 TO 2 CUPS PACKED)

4 SMALL CLOVES GARLIC

1/3 TO 1/2 CUP PINE NUTS

ABOUT 1/2 TEASPOON COARSE SEA SALT

1/2 CUP GRATED PARMIGIANO-REGGIANO CHEESE,
PLUS EXTRA FOR SERVING

ABOUT 1/2 CUP EXTRA-VIRGIN OLIVE OIL

SALT

1 POUND DRIED LINGUINE

Preparation:

1 To make the pesto, in a large mortar, crush and grind together the basil, garlic, pine nuts, and sea salt until a paste forms. Use a steady, circular motion to grind them together. Work in the 1/2 cup cheese, then begin adding the olive oil—first only in a trickle—gradually working it into a paste. Keep grinding and stirring with the pestle as you add the oil. The sauce is ready when it is thick, smooth, and of uniform consistency.

2 Bring a large saucepan filled with water to a boil. Add salt to taste and the pasta, stir well, and cook until *al dente*, 8 to 10 minutes or according to package instructions. Drain and place in a serving bowl. Add the pesto and toss well, then add more cheese and olive oil to taste and again toss well. The starch of the pasta should blend fully with the pesto sauce. Serve immediately.

Spoleto

ntil the late 1950s, when composer Giancarlo Menotti established his Festival of Two Worlds here, Spoleto was virtually unknown beyond Italy's borders. This medieval hill town lies in the landlocked region of Umbria, north of Rome and southeast of Tuscany. It is an area blessed with high mountains, deep valleys, and, according to regional partisans, some of Italy's most innovative cooking, much of it built on such local ingredients as pork, wild asparagus, black truffles, green lentils, and pecorino cheese.

Spoleto has a long history, and its many ancient Roman structures, both standing and in ruins, are proof of it. Its amphitheater is nearly two-thirds the size of the Colosseum in Rome, and its first-century theater is still used today. But it is the elegant, nearly one-thousand-year-old *duomo*, fronted by a secluded *piazza*, and set against a backdrop of Umbrian hills, that inevitably turns heads. Its facade is of Byzantine-inspired mosaics, its frescoes are by Filippo Lippi and Pinturicchio, and its scope is grand—and unforgettable.

Northeast of Spoleto lies the beautiful and untouristed area of Valnerina, a landscape marked with Roman bridges and ruins and site of the oldest abbey in Umbria, the eighth-century San Pietro in Valle, above the village of Coloponte. It is also where trout and small crayfish are pulled from a network of narrow canals in the town of Scheggino, and where black truffles are mined by serious hunters and their well-trained dogs.

Umbria is serene, well watered, rich in forests and dales, and home to not only lovely Spoleto, but also Perugia, Assisi, Orvieto, Gubbio, and dozens of other inviting towns. Local cooks remain faithful to the area's rustic, natural *cucina*, serving such appealing fare as *porchetta* (suckling pig seasoned with garlic and wild fennel); squab cooked with olives; and *tegamaccio*, a mixed-fish stew traditionally made with the catch from large Lake Trasimeno.

TRUFFLED OMELET
FRITTATA AL TARTUFO

Pricy black truffles—*tartufi neri*—are a specialty of Umbria, particularly around the towns of Norcia and Spoleto, where they are hunted in nearby forests. In the kitchen, these prized fungi are grated, combined with cream, and tossed with fettuccine; made into a sauce for beef fillet; or whisked into eggs, as they are here.

6 TO 8 EGGS

2 TABLESPOONS TOMATO SAUCE

2 TABLESPOONS HEAVY CREAM

2 TO 3 TABLESPOONS GRATED BLACK TRUFFLE

SALT

2 LARGE SPOONFULS EXTRA-VIRGIN OLIVE OIL

Preparation:

1 Break the eggs into a bowl and whisk to combine the yolks and whites. Add the tomato sauce, cream, truffle, and salt to taste and whisk to blend.

2 In a large frying pan over medium heat, warm the olive oil. Pour in the egg mixture and cook, stirring constantly, until the eggs are just beginning to set but are still quite soft and creamy, about 2 minutes. Be careful not to overcook. The consistency should be of very soft scrambled eggs. Remove from the heat. Spoon onto warmed individual plates and serve at once.

Alto Adige

ach year, tens of thousands of European tourists pass through Alto Adige, Italy's northernmost province, on their way to the Italian Lakes or the sandy beaches of the Mediterranean, usually never pausing to take in the local sights. They are missing the spectacle of the Alps and the Dolomites, of unspoiled lakes and pristine rivers, of leafy apple orchards and terraced vineyards, of wood-paneled taverns and hearty meals.

In the past, before World War I, the area was known as South Tyrol, the result of its domination by the Counts of Tyrol during the Middle Ages and later under the Austrian Empire. The Adige River cuts through the center of the province, creating fertile valleys in which wheat, corn, rye, oats, and barley are cultivated and dairy and beef cattle are raised. The pig is important here, too, being the source of one of the province's best-known products, *speck*, smoked pork leg. So, too, is wine, which has been produced for more than two millennia. The best wine district, which lies in the south, is traversed by the lovely twenty-five-mile-long Strada del Vino (Wine Road), with vineyards to visit posted along the way.

In the prosperous capital, Bolzano (Bozen), both Italian and German are spoken. Piazza Walther, the social heart of the town, is named for locally born Walther von der Vogelweide, the most celebrated medieval poet in the German language and a troubadour who roamed the countryside, serenading the castle-bound with lyrics of love and chivalry.

The cities and towns of Alto Adige suffer from a split personality, part Italian and part Teutonic. Restaurant menus list dishes in both German and Italian, such as *gulasch di manzo* and *Rindsgulasch* (beef stew with alpine herbs) and *fritelle di mele* and *Apfelkuchel* (apple fritters). Even the excellent local wines—dry whites and light reds—many of which are exported to Germany and Austria, carry labels in both languages.

BREAD AND SPINACH GNOCCHI
GNOCCHI DI PANE E SPINACI

SERVES FOUR

Gnocchi, plump little dumplings of various sizes, can be based on a variety of different ingredients, from potatoes to semolina flour to chestnut flour to cornmeal to pumpkin. Here, bread is the base for egg-sized gnocchi dressed with a simple topping of melted butter, Parmigiano-Reggiano cheese, and a scattering of chives.

10 TABLESPOONS UNSALTED BUTTER

1 YELLOW ONION, FINELY CHOPPED

3/4 POUND SPINACH, BOILED, DRAINED, SQUEEZED DRY, AND CHOPPED

1 TABLESPOON FINELY CHOPPED GARLIC

1/2 POUND STALE COARSE COUNTRY BREAD, CRUSTS REMOVED AND CUT INTO CUBES (3 TO 4 CUPS)

2 TABLESPOONS ALL-PURPOSE FLOUR

1 1/2 CUPS MILK

3 EGGS

1/2 CUP GRATED PARMIGIANO-REGGIANO CHEESE

SALT AND FRESHLY GROUND BLACK PEPPER

CHOPPED FRESH CHIVES FOR GARNISH

Preparation:

1 In a frying pan over medium heat, melt 4 tablespoons of the butter. Add the onion and sauté until golden, 5 to 8 minutes. Add the spinach and garlic and continue to sauté for 2 to 3 minutes to blend the flavors. Remove from the heat and let cool.

2 In a bowl, combine the bread, flour, milk, eggs, 2 tablespoons of the cheese, and salt and pepper to taste and mix well. Add the spinach mixture and again mix well. Let stand for 30 minutes to allow the bread to soften and the mixture to bind. (You can prepare this mixture in the morning, cover, and refrigerate, and then continue just before serving in the evening.)

3 Dampen your hands to prevent sticking, then use them to shape the mixture into ovals about the size of eggs. You should have 12 to 16 gnocchi.

4 Bring a large pot filled with water to a gentle boil. Add salt to taste and the gnocchi, adjust the heat so the gnocchi poach gently, and cook until done, 10 to 15 minutes. Cut into a gnocchi to test for doneness.

5 Just before the gnocchi are ready, melt the remaining 6 tablespoons butter in a pan over medium heat until hot and foamy.

6 Drain the gnocchi and divide evenly among warmed individual plates. Sprinkle with the chives and drizzle with the butter. Top evenly with the remaining 6 tablespoons cheese and serve at once.

Udine

The region of Friuli, bordered by the Veneto, Austria, Slovenia, and the Adriatic Sea, is a study in contrast: alpine in the north and flattening to a wide plain in the south. It is one of the least visited areas of Italy, and at the same time is responsible for some of its best wines and finest foods. Here you will find the country estate of the last Doge of Venice and exquisite Roman mosaics in ancient Aquileia, as well as meadows thick with wild herbs and greens gathered for the local cooking.

The handsome community of Udine, with its Renaissance Piazza della Libertà, shows off Friuli—and the hardworking, friendly Friulani who live here—at its best. The city is Roman in origin, but it was conquered by the Venetians in 1420, who shared their fortunes with them until the Napoleonic era. It then came under the rule of the Hapsburgs until 1866, when it was reunited with Italy. Echoes of Venice are everywhere. Its city hall recalls the Doge's Palace in Piazza San Marco, and its clock tower, which rises from a nearby loggia, has two dark bronze Moors striking the hour, much like the famed *torre* in San Marco.

Among the wonderful foods and beverages found in Friuli are mountain cheeses, yellow peaches, and fat sausages. But the area's greatest culinary accolades are reserved for the world-famous violin-shaped San Daniele prosciutto, made in the town of the same name, where the air is ideal for curing.

The *cucina* of Friuli is rustic and distinctive, from its *gnocchi di susina* (stuffed with a prune) and *frico* (cheese fritters) to its *brovada* (turnips with sausage) and *gubana*, a cake filled with nuts, cocoa, candied fruit, spices, and liqueur. Local wine cellars house particularly fine regional whites, including bottles of Tocai, Pinot Grigio, and Riesling Renano, while Friuli's potent grappa delivers welcome heat during the region's cold winter nights.

The most celebrated of all Friulian foods is *prosciutto di San Daniele*, made in a small town about fifteen miles from Udine. The legs of pork, which average about twenty-eight pounds and always have the hoof intact (to prevent the lower portion of the leg from drying out), are salted and left for about two weeks, and then pressed into their attractive violin shape and hung to mature for a little over a year.

PASTA WITH RABBIT RAGÙ
MALTAGLIATI AL RAGÙ DE CONIGLIO

SERVES FOUR

In Udine, this dish is typically made with a pasta called *maltagliati*, literally "poorly cut." The name comes from a time when the Italian housewife regularly made ravioli and tortellini, and the strips of dough that were left over after cutting out the filled pastas would be saved and tossed with sauce for another meal. Other short pasta shapes can be used here

1 RABBIT, 2 ½ POUNDS, QUARTERED

SALT AND FRESHLY GROUND BLACK PEPPER

EXTRA-VIRGIN OLIVE OIL FOR PANFRYING

3 FRESH ROSEMARY SPRIGS

2 FRESH OR 1 DRIED BAY LEAF

3 OR 4 FRESH SAGE LEAVES

2 YELLOW ONIONS, CHOPPED

3 CARROTS, PEELED AND CHOPPED

3 CELERY STALKS, CHOPPED

1 CUP DRY RED WINE

4 CUPS BEEF STOCK (PAGE 159)

1 POUND DRIED *MALTAGLIATI* OR OTHER SHORT PASTA

¾ POUND CHERRY TOMATOES, STEMMED AND CHOPPED

UNSALTED BUTTER

GRATED PARMIGIANO-REGGIANO CHEESE FOR SERVING

Preparation:

1 Sprinkle the rabbit pieces with salt and pepper. In a large, deep frying pan over medium-high heat, warm the olive oil. Add the rabbit pieces and fry, turning as necessary, until golden on all sides. Meanwhile, tie together the rosemary sprigs and bay and sage leaves to make a bouquet garni.

2 Reduce the heat to medium and add the onions, carrots, celery, and bouquet garni to the pan. Cook, stirring, until golden, about 5 minutes. Add ½ cup of the wine, stir well, and allow it to evaporate. Add about 1 cup of the beef stock, reduce the heat to low, and simmer the rabbit, uncovered, until the rabbit is very tender. The stock will evaporate during cooking. As it does, add more stock, a ladleful at a time.

3 Remove the pan from the heat, and lift out the rabbit pieces. When they are cool enough to handle, slide the meat off the bones. It should come off quickly and easily. Discard the bones and shred the meat into little strings. Return the meat to the pan. Discard the herb bouquet.

4 Bring a large pot of water to a boil. Add salt to taste and the pasta, stir well, and cook until not quite *al dente*, about 8 minutes or a couple of minutes less than the package instructions.

5 Meanwhile, return the frying pan to medium heat and add the tomatoes. Mix well, add the remaining ½ cup red wine and a little butter to taste. Stir again and wait for the wine to evaporate and the ingredients to blend.

6 Drain the pasta and add it to the sauce. Stir well and allow the pasta to finish cooking in the sauce. Be careful not to overcook it.

7 Divide the pasta among warmed individual plates, sprinkle with a little cheese—or pass the cheese at the table—and serve at once.

This fifteenth-century Venetian castle is now home to vintners who produce some of the region's finest red wines.

Lido di Jésolo

ying twelve miles northeast of Venice, Lido di Jésolo is first and foremost a sandy beach, a place where Italians and their European neighbors come to soak up the sunshine and swim in the Adriatic. At the height of summer, the beach is a swirl of activity, with families setting off with snorkels and fins to explore the shallow waters, and young men playing hard-fought yet friendly games of soccer near the shore. And when the heat is at its most sizzling, the beachside *gelato* man cannot scoop the ice cream quickly enough.

Beyond the pale gold strand lies a fertile plain populated with a treasure trove of villas, castles, and Roman ruins and of farmlands planted with grapevines. A Roman road, dating from the first century, was unearthed here in the 1960s, along with countless other discoveries—portals, mosaics, burial chambers—all of them predating the establishment of Venice. Indeed, people who once lived in this area fell subject to conquerors and sought refuge on the islands that now make up the world-famous city of canals. They reportedly carried with them the stones of their destroyed communities to create a new one.

Visitors who grow weary of the beach and of pursuing ancient ruins in the countryside find Venice the perfect antidote. Once there, they board gondolas in search of legendary monuments, of course, but also of homey *trattorias* where *pasta alla vongole* and glasses of pale, refreshing Soave are enjoyed amid the lilting dialect of the Venetians.

OCTOPUS SALAD
INSALATA DI POLPI

SERVES FOUR

Here, when you cook the octopus for the salad, you are making the stock for *zuppa* at the same time. Pour a dry white Veneto wine, such as Bianco di Custoza or a Soave, to accompany the salad.

FOR THE OCTOPUS:

1 LARGE OCTOPUS

1 YELLOW ONION, HALVED

2 CELERY STALKS, HALVED

2 CARROTS, HALVED

1 LEMON, HALVED

2 QUARTS PLUS 3 CUPS WATER

FOR THE SALAD:

2 CELERY STALKS, CHOPPED

2 CARROTS, PEELED AND CHOPPED

EXTRA-VIRGIN OLIVE OIL FOR DRIZZLING

1 LEMON, HALVED

2 TABLESPOONS CHOPPED FRESH
FLAT-LEAF PARSLEY

SALT AND FRESHLY GROUND BLACK PEPPER

Preparation:

1 Octopus is typically sold precleaned. If it has not been cleaned, invert it—much like you might turn a sock inside out—and remove the beak and viscera from the mouth, including the ink sac, rinsing well under running cold water. To tenderize it, bring a large pot of water to a boil and, holding the octopus by its mantle, dip it into the boiling water for about 10 seconds and pull it out. Let it cool slightly, then dip it again. Repeat 1 or 2 more times.

2 Place the octopus, onion, celery, carrots, and water to cover generously in a large pot and bring to a boil. Partially cover the pot and cook until the octopus is tender, about 1 hour. Transfer the octopus to a large platter and set aside to cool. Strain the resulting stock and discard the solids. Measure out the stock and set aside 4 cups to use for making the fish soup (page 70).

3 To make the salad, cut the octopus into bite-sized pieces and place in a serving bowl. Add the celery and carrots and toss to mix. Drizzle with a generous amount of olive oil and squeeze the lemon halves to extract the juice. Toss well. Add the parsley, season to taste with salt and pepper, and toss again to mix thoroughly. Serve at once, or cover and refrigerate until serving.

FISH SOUP
ZUPPA DI PESCE

SERVES FOUR

In Italy, this soup calls for scampi, which are the tail sections of small members of the lobster family known elsewhere as lobsterettes, langoustines, and Dublin Bay prawns. If you cannot find them, use jumbo shrimp or prawns in their place. If you are making the soup but not the octopus antipasto, you can prepare the stock by using the same instructions and substituting 3 to 4 pounds fish frames (skeletons), including heads with gills removed, for the octopus.

FOR THE SOUP:

14 OUNCES SQUID

16 CLAMS

16 MUSSELS

8 SCAMPI

1/2 POUND SHRIMP IN THE SHELL

1 POUND FRESH BONELESS TUNA STEAK

EXTRA-VIRGIN OLIVE OIL FOR SAUTÉING

4 CLOVES GARLIC, FINELY CHOPPED

1 YELLOW ONION, CHOPPED

SALT AND FRESHLY GROUND BLACK PEPPER

1/4 CUP BRANDY

3/4 CUP DRY WHITE WINE

1 CUP CHERRY TOMATOES, STEMMED
AND CHOPPED

4 CUPS STOCK FROM OCTOPUS SALAD (PAGE 68)

2 TABLESPOONS CHOPPED FRESH
FLAT-LEAF PARSLEY

RED PEPPER FLAKES

FOR THE CROSTINI:

8 THIN SLICES COARSE COUNTRY BREAD, TOASTED

1 CLOVE GARLIC

EXTRA-VIRGIN OLIVE OIL FOR DRIZZLING

Preparation:

1 To make the soup, first clean the squid: cut off the tentacles just above the eyes. Squeeze the base of the tentacles to pop out the hard beak. Rinse the tentacles well and set aside whole. Pull out and discard the cartilage-like "quill" from the body, then rinse the body well, discarding the entrails. Carefully pull off the thin, mottled skin that covers the body and rinse the body again. Cut the body into inch-wide rings and set aside with the tentacles.

2 Scrub the clams and mussels well, discarding those that do not close to the touch. Debeard the mussels. Soak the clams in salted water for 15 minutes to help rid them of sand. Drain and set aside with the mussels. Rinse the scampi and shrimp and set aside. Cut the tuna into chunks.

3 In a large pot over medium heat, warm a little olive oil. Add half of the garlic and all of the onion and sauté until beginning to soften, 2 to 3 minutes. Add the tuna, squid rings and tentacles, scampi, and shrimp and cook, stirring to prevent sticking, for 1 minute. Season with salt and pepper and add the brandy and 1/4 cup of the wine. Cook for a couple of minutes until the liquids reduce. Add the tomatoes, stock, parsley, and red pepper flakes to taste and stir. Reduce the heat to low, cover, and cook at a gentle simmer for about 15 minutes. Do not boil.

4 Meanwhile, place 2 frying pans on the stove over medium heat. Add a little oil to each pan, then divide the remaining garlic and the remaining wine (1/4 cup to each) between them. Place the mussels in one pan and the clams in the other, cover both pans, and cook, shaking the pans occasionally, until the shellfish open, about 5 minutes. Remove from the heat and discard any clams or mussels that failed to open. Drain off the liquid from the mussels (some diners find it to be too fishy), but do not drain the clams. Set aside.

5 To make the *crostini*, rub each toasted bread slice with the garlic clove (or grate the garlic over the slices), then drizzle with olive oil.

6 Taste the soup and adjust the seasoning. Divide the soup evenly among warmed individual bowls. Add 4 mussels (drained) and 4 clams (with their liquid) to each bowl. Arrange 2 *crostini* in each bowl and serve at once.

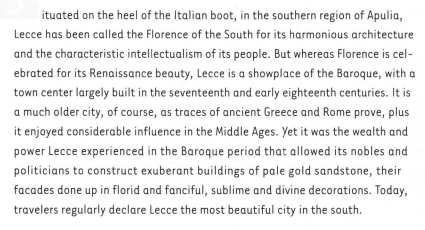

Lecce

Situated on the heel of the Italian boot, in the southern region of Apulia, Lecce has been called the Florence of the South for its harmonious architecture and the characteristic intellectualism of its people. But whereas Florence is celebrated for its Renaissance beauty, Lecce is a showplace of the Baroque, with a town center largely built in the seventeenth and early eighteenth centuries. It is a much older city, of course, as traces of ancient Greece and Rome prove, plus it enjoyed considerable influence in the Middle Ages. Yet it was the wealth and power Lecce experienced in the Baroque period that allowed its nobles and politicians to construct exuberant buildings of pale gold sandstone, their facades done up in florid and fanciful, sublime and divine decorations. Today, travelers regularly declare Lecce the most beautiful city in the south.

Although Lecce, which stands almost at the midpoint of the Salentine peninsula, is not on the sea, it is close to it, and its tables often feature fresh fish pulled from the surrounding waters. The low, rock-studded coastline sports a handful of ports, including Otranto on the Adriatic, where the local market displays fish from nearby waters and ferries set sail for Greece. Gallipoli, on the Ionian coast, has a charming old quarter, whitewashed houses, and weathered fishermen at work in the small harbor. Away from the sea, locals speak of the productive vineyards, the source of Salice Salentino, recognized as a respectable, moderately priced wine far beyond the region's borders.

Although the city of Lecce is considered an architectural masterpiece, the food of Lecce—and the rest of Apulia— presents a less lavish profile. Most dishes begin with olive oil, and grains and vegetables are central to the diet, with meat typically playing a secondary role. The region is particularly known for its hearty breads with a chewy crust and flaxen crumb, especially those baked in the town of Altamura, on Apulia's central plain.

TOMATO SAUCE
SALSA DI POMODORO

SERVES FOUR

Here is a tomato sauce to make any *nonna*—grandmother—proud. It is quick and easy and is wonderful tossed with fresh or dried pasta. A food mill makes fast work of the skins and seeds. Choose whichever type of tomato is ripest, meatiest, and has the most substantial heft for its size.

3 ⅓ POUNDS CHERRY, PLUM, OR OTHER TOMATOES

5 TABLESPOONS EXTRA-VIRGIN OLIVE OIL

1 LARGE YELLOW ONION, CHOPPED

5 OR 6 FRESH BASIL LEAVES

SALT

Preparation:

1 Fill a bowl with cold water. Then, one at a time if using large tomatoes, or a few at a time if using cherry tomatoes, submerge the tomatoes and squeeze. This will release the excess juice and many of the seeds and prevent the tomatoes from splattering in the process. Transfer the tomatoes to a heavy saucepan.

2 When all the tomatoes have been crushed, add the olive oil, onion, basil, and salt to taste and place over medium heat. Bring to a boil, cover, reduce the heat to a simmer, and cook until the onion is soft and the tomatoes have broken down, about 15 minutes. Remove from the heat and pass through a food mill placed over bowl. (This will remove any remaining seeds.)

3 Transfer the tomatoes to the pan and return to medium heat. Simmer for about 5 minutes to blend the flavors, then use as desired.

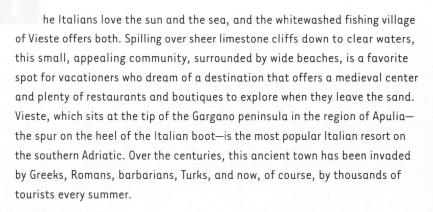

Vieste

he Italians love the sun and the sea, and the whitewashed fishing village of Vieste offers both. Spilling over sheer limestone cliffs down to clear waters, this small, appealing community, surrounded by wide beaches, is a favorite spot for vacationers who dream of a destination that offers a medieval center and plenty of restaurants and boutiques to explore when they leave the sand. Vieste, which sits at the tip of the Gargano peninsula in the region of Apulia—the spur on the heel of the Italian boot—is the most popular Italian resort on the southern Adriatic. Over the centuries, this ancient town has been invaded by Greeks, Romans, barbarians, Turks, and now, of course, by thousands of tourists every summer.

South of Vieste, along a coastline punctuated with picturesque coves, stands Mattinata, a cubist's dream of rectangular white houses overlooking the sea and a broad plain. Inland, past groves of olive and almond trees, the traveler comes upon one of the leading pilgrimage sites in Italy, the town of Monte Sant'Angelo with its legendary ninth-century castle and the sanctuary of Saint Michael. Pilgrims, among them Thomas Aquinas, Catherine of Siena, and Saint Francis, have journeyed here over the centuries to stand at the spot where Saint Michael the Archangel is said to have appeared to shepherds in the fifth century, leaving behind his red cloak as proof of his visit. The town itself, which has preserved its traditional folklore and customs, is an appealing maze of narrow, steep streets.

With a coastline that stretches hundreds of miles, Apulia offers local cooks a varied catch for the table: red mullet, John Dory, monkfish, salmon, octopus, squid, clams, mussels, sardines, anchovies, and more. They use this bounty in nearly every course, tossing it with pasta, simmering it in soups and stews, grilling it, baking it, frying it, or boiling it and serving it cold with a squeeze of lemon and a splash of olive oil.

ORECCHIETTE WITH BROCCOLI RABE AND ANCHOVY SAUCE
ORECCHIETTE CON CIMA DI RAPA

SERVES FOUR

A member of the mustard family, the sharply flavored broccoli rabe is primarily eaten by southern Italians, especially Apulians. Also known as *cima di rapa*, *broccoli di rape*, and *rapini*, it is commonly sautéed and served as a *contorno*, often as an accompaniment to a *secondo* of grilled sausages or lamb chops, or it is tossed with anchovies, garlic, and the famed local pasta, *orecchiette*—little ears.

Preparation:

1 Bring a large saucepan filled with water to a boil. Add salt to taste and the pasta, stir well, and cook until *al dente*, about 3 minutes for fresh pasta and 10 minutes for dried pasta, or according to package instructions. Add the broccoli rabe to the boiling pasta for the last 2 minutes of cooking time.

2 Meanwhile, in a large frying pan over medium-high heat, warm the olive oil. Add the garlic, chili peppers, and anchovies and cook, stirring often, until the garlic is fragrant and golden and the anchovies have "melted" into the oil, about 3 minutes.

3 Drain the pasta and greens, reserving a ladleful of the cooking water. Add the pasta and greens to the frying pan and stir and toss to mix. Add the reserved cooking water as needed to moisten the pasta and toss well so that the olive oil, starch from the pasta, and cooking water form a blended sauce.

4 Transfer to a warmed serving bowl or individual plates and serve immediately.

SALT

1 POUND FRESH OR DRIED *ORECCHIETTE*

2 ¼ POUNDS YOUNG, TENDER BROCCOLI RABE, TOUGH STEMS REMOVED AND CUT INTO 2-INCH LENGTHS

2 TO 3 TABLESPOONS EXTRA-VIRGIN OLIVE OIL

2 CLOVES GARLIC, CRUSHED

1 OR 2 SMALL DRIED CHILI PEPPERS, OR TO TASTE

7 OUNCES ANCHOVY FILLETS IN OLIVE OIL, DRAINED AND CHOPPED

FAVA BEANS WITH DANDELION GREENS
FAVETTA E CICORIA

Fava beans are a pantry staple in Apulia, where they are often combined with wild greens that grow in the meadows and on the hillsides. Here, they are puréed and combined with jagged-edged, pleasantly bitter dandelion greens that have been simply boiled and drained. Already peeled, dried favas are sometimes available, in which case you will need half the amount indicated. You will still need to soak them, however, to shorten the cooking time.

2 CUPS DRIED FAVA BEANS

2 CLOVES GARLIC

2 BAY LEAVES

SALT

FOR THE *CROSTINI*:

8 SLICES COARSE COUNTRY BREAD

2 CLOVES GARLIC, CRUSHED

EXTRA-VIRGIN OLIVE OIL FOR DRIZZLING

2 1/2 POUNDS DANDELION GREENS, TOUGH STEMS REMOVED

EXTRA-VIRGIN OLIVE OIL FOR DRIZZLING

Preparation:

1 Pick over the beans, rinse well, place in a bowl, and add water to cover. Let stand overnight. The next day, drain and slip off the loosened skins from the beans; they should come off easily.

2 Transfer the beans to a saucepan and add the garlic, bay leaves, and water just to cover. Bring to a boil over medium-high heat, reduce the heat to a simmer and cook, uncovered, until the beans are very tender and have broken down to a coarse purée, about 1 1/2 hours. If the beans begin to dry out during cooking, add boiling water as needed to keep them moist. When the beans are ready, discard the bay leaves and mash as needed to create a thick purée. Season with salt and keep warm.

3 To make the crostini, preheat the broiler, or prepare a fire in a charcoal grill. Broil or grill the bread, turning once, until lightly browned on both sides, just a couple of minutes. Remove from the broiler or grill and immediately rub each slice on both sides with the crushed garlic. Drizzle lightly with olive oil.

4 Meanwhile, bring a large pot of water to a boil and add salt to taste and the dandelion greens. Boil until tender, 3 to 7 minutes. The timing will depend on the age of the greens. Drain well.

5 Place the dandelion greens in the middle of a serving dish and spoon the fava purée around them. Arrange the *crostini* on the dish and drizzle olive oil over all. Serve at once.

Lanciano

The Abruzzo, which is bordered by the Adriatic on the east, the Marches on the north, and Molise to the south, is defined by the wild beauty of the Apennines, whose peaks dominate its landscape. This rugged terrain allows limited room for agriculture and has kept population pockets relatively small. Despite the restrictions imposed by nature, Lanciano, a bustling yet little-known community that wears its charm on nearly every doorstep, was an important medieval marketplace for wool and other fabrics, attracting merchants from all over Europe to its annual fairs. Today, the town is divided into two parts, the old and the modern, and evidence of its mercantile heyday are visible in the church of Santa Maria Maggiore, built in the thirteenth century and altered in the fourteenth and fifteenth centuries, and in the Porta San Biagio.

One of the most scenic drives in all of Italy begins in Lanciano and ends at the Roccaraso, some 50 winding miles south, near the Abruzzo National Park. The park itself is large, about 120 square miles, and packed with countless wonders of nature. The native chamois and brown bear of the Abruzzo are here, as are lynx, wolves, deer, and countless bird varieties, all protected from hunters' guns. Forests of yews, oaks, and other trees and meadows of spring flowers and wild herbs beguile the most jaded naturalist. The wise hiker picks up a trail map at the visitors' center to discover what unique beauties this national park, Italy's second largest, holds.

Much of the Abruzzese economy depends on agriculture. Vegetables, corn, wheat, and herbs and spices, including saffron, are important crops. Sheep are raised in the mountainous interior for meat and milk, while tables in the coastal provinces are laden with seafood from the Adriatic. Throughout the region, however, cooks depend on peperoncini (chilies) to season everything from salumi (cold cuts) to pasta sauces to brodetto, a fish stew that varies with each seaside town.

PORCINI SOUP
ZUPPA DI PORCINI

SERVES FOUR

Robust, woodsy, earthy—the *porcino*—little pig in Italian—is the Italian cook's favorite mushroom, used both fresh and dried. Following a spring rain, foragers in the Abruzzo are out in the countryside in force, bent over gathering these prized fungi. This simple soup shows off the meaty mushrooms beautifully. Early in the day, prepare it up to the point where the egg yolks are added, then finish it just before serving. The flavor improves when the soup sits for a few hours.

Preparation:

1 In a saucepan over medium-high heat, warm the olive oil. Add the garlic and sauté until golden, about 3 minutes. Add the porcini, season with salt, and cook, stirring until the moisture is released from the mushrooms and evaporates, 4 to 5 minutes.

2 Meanwhile, cut the butter into 3 or 4 pieces and roll each in a little flour. Add the pieces to the pan (they will help thicken the soup), stir briefly, then add 1 or 2 tablespoons parsley. Pour in the stock and bring to a boil. Reduce the heat to medium-low and simmer for about 20 minutes to blend the flavors.

3 Remove the pan from the heat and add the egg yolks to the soup. Return the pan to the stove and heat through, about 1 minute. The eggs should just set. Do not allow to boil.

4 Ladle into warmed bowls and sprinkle with 1 tablespoon parsley, divided evenly. Scatter a few croutons on top and serve immediately.

2 TABLESPOONS EXTRA-VIRGIN OLIVE OIL

2 CLOVES GARLIC, CHOPPED

10 OUNCES FRESH PORCINI, BRUSHED CLEAN AND CHOPPED

SALT

2 TABLESPOONS UNSALTED BUTTER

ALL-PURPOSE FLOUR, AS NEEDED

2 OR 3 TABLESPOONS CHOPPED FRESH FLAT-LEAF PARSLEY

3 ¼ CUPS VEGETABLE STOCK (PAGE 158)

2 EGG YOLKS, LIGHTLY BEATEN

CROUTONS (PAGE 158)

LAMB WITH EGGS AND PECORINO CHEESE
AGNELLO CACIO E UOVO

SERVES FOUR

Lamb is a favored meat in Abruzzo, and in the past, each September shepherds would drive their flocks from the region's highlands south to Apulia to better grazing lands. Even today, some shepherds migrate considerable distances every year to ensure a steady diet for their charges. This dish is a classic of the region.

2 TO 3 TABLESPOONS EXTRA-VIRGIN OLIVE OIL

1/2 YELLOW ONION, CHOPPED

1/2 RED BELL PEPPER, SEEDED AND CHOPPED

1 3/4 POUNDS BONELESS TENDER LAMB, CUT INTO CUBES

SALT

3/4 CUP DRY WHITE WINE

1/4 TO 1/3 CUP WATER

2 FRESH ROSEMARY SPRIGS

3 OR 4 EGGS

1 1/2 CUPS GRATED PECORINO CHEESE

1 TABLESPOON CHOPPED FRESH FLAT-LEAF PARSLEY

Preparation:

1 In a large sauté pan or flameproof earthenware casserole over high heat, warm the olive oil. Add the onion and red pepper and cook, stirring until golden brown, 3 to 5 minutes. Add the lamb pieces, season with salt, and brown evenly on all sides.

2 Pour in the wine and deglaze the pan, stirring to dislodge any browned bits stuck to the pan bottom. Reduce the wine by half. Add the water and rosemary, cover, reduce the heat to medium-low, and cook until the lamb is tender, 30 to 40 minutes.

3 In a bowl, beat the eggs with the cheese. Uncover the lamb mixture, pour the cheese mixture evenly over the lamb, stir to combine, reduce the heat to low, and cook for about 2 minutes just until the eggs are set.

4 Sprinkle with the parsley and serve at once.

L' Aquila thrives in a mountain setting, and its central market, in the *piazza* that fronts the *duomo*, overflows with crops harvested in the valleys below the town. One of the best ways to sample the local dishes is to attend a *panarda*, a traditional Abruzzese feast held to celebrate an important event—a wedding, a saint's day, an anniversary—and classically consisting of thirty-six dishes but sometimes many more.

L'Aquila

The most important city in the Abruzzo, L' Aquila rose in a swirl of numbers. It was founded by Frederick II in 1240, who, according to legend, decided to relocate the people who inhabited the ninety-nine castles, villages, and hamlets in the area to a new site. The resulting city was laid out with ninety-nine wards to represent each of its original communities, and outfitted with ninety-nine fountains, ninety-nine churches, and ninety-nine squares. (If this is indeed more than legend, many of the early structures have been lost to history.) Today, the most famous monument in L' Aquila is the Fontana delle 99 Cannelle—the Fountain of 99 Spouts—built in the thirteenth century as the city's main water supply and remodeled in the Renaissance. The marble fountain stands in a lovely rose-and-ivory checkered square near a medieval portal. Another reminder of the city's origins: every evening the bell in the main *piazza* rings out ninety-nine times.

During the 1800s, the number of sheep raised at any one time on the barren, rocky landscape of Abruzzo was as much as twenty million, and L' Aquila was the center of the wool trade. Today, agriculture is still important, with the tending of sheep, goats, and cattle and the cultivation of various vegetables, herbs, and olives. But the region's most specialized crop is saffron, the reddish orange stigma of a variety of purple crocus. The best saffron comes from the town of Navelli, which lies southeast of L' Aquila and is also famous for its chickpeas.

RABBIT WITH SAFFRON AND MUSHROOMS

CONIGLIO CON ZAFFERANO E FUNGHI

SERVES FOUR

The milk is used in this recipe for two reasons: It ensures that the rabbit cooks to a tender and moist finish, and it complements the saffron, which turns the liquid a lovely sunny gold and subtly perfumes the whole dish.

Preparation:

1 Preheat the oven to 375°F.

2 In an ovenproof Dutch oven or other heavy pot over high heat, warm the olive oil. Add the garlic and sauté until well browned, about 3 minutes. Remove the garlic and discard. (The oil will be flavored with garlic.)

3 Add the rabbit pieces to the pan and sauté on all sides until golden brown, 2 to 3 minutes. Add the mushrooms and sauté until they release their liquid and the liquid evaporates, 4 to 5 minutes. Add the wine and allow it to reduce by half.

4 Meanwhile, cut the butter into 3 or 4 pieces and roll each in a little flour. Add the milk and then the butter pieces to the pan (they will help to thicken the sauce) and stir well. Sprinkle with saffron and season with salt. Cook, stirring, for 2 minutes longer, then cover and place in the oven until the rabbit is tender, 15 to 20 minutes.

5 Transfer to a warmed serving dish or individual plates and serve at once.

2 TO 3 TABLESPOONS EXTRA-VIRGIN OLIVE OIL

2 CLOVES GARLIC, CRUSHED

1 RABBIT, ABOUT 2 1/4 POUNDS, CUT INTO SERVING PIECES

2 POUNDS FRESH CULTIVATED WHITE MUSHROOMS, BRUSHED CLEAN AND QUARTERED

1 1/2 CUPS DRY WHITE WINE

2 1/2 TABLESPOONS UNSALTED BUTTER

ALL-PURPOSE FLOUR FOR DUSTING

1 1/2 CUPS MILK

SPRINKLING OF POWDERED SAFFRON

SALT

PASTA WITH RICOTTA AND SAFFRON
MALTAGLIATI CON RICOTTA E ZAFFERANO

SERVES FOUR

Saffron was used in the kitchens of ancient Rome, but then disappeared for the most part from Italy until the twelfth century, when it reappeared in Venice. Today, it is found on spice shelves throughout the country and used in such dishes as risotto in Milan, in fish stew on the Adriatic, in small dumplings in Sardinia, and in this ricotta sauce for pasta in Abruzzo.

SALT

1 POUND FRESH *MALTAGLIATI* OR OTHER SHORT HOMEMADE PASTA

1 1/2 CUPS MILK

2 TABLESPOONS HEAVY CREAM

1 ROUNDED CUP (8 OUNCES) RICOTTA CHEESE

SPRINKLING OF POWDERED SAFFRON

Preparation:

1 Bring a large saucepan filled with water to a boil. Add salt to taste and the pasta, stir well, and cook until nearly *al dente*, about 2 minutes.

2 Meanwhile, in a large frying pan over high heat, combine the milk and cream and bring to a simmer. Allow to reduce slightly.

3 When the pasta is ready, drain and add to the milk mixture. Continue cooking and stirring over high heat, allowing the milk to reduce a bit more and the starch of the pasta to thicken the sauce. Add the ricotta in large spoonfuls, sprinkle with the saffron, season with salt, and cook briefly, stirring, to heat the ricotta through. These final steps should take only a couple of minutes.

4 Transfer to a warmed serving dish or individual plates and serve immediately.

Along the Conero Riviera, south of Ancona, steep, white limestone cliffs reach right down to the sea.

Conero Riviera

The region known as the Marches lies between the mountains and the sea—the Apennines and the Adriatic—and shares its borders with Umbria, Abruzzo, and Emilia-Romagna. The emerald landscape that travels down from the mountain peaks ends in a series of dazzling coves, bays, and beaches. The Conero Riviera just south of the crescent-shaped harbor of Ancona and backed by the limestone peaks of Mount Conero, is arguably the northern Adriatic's most stunning stretch of bathing beaches.

On the road south of Ancona stands the little resort town of Portonovo, with a lovely eleventh-century church and a row of seaside cafés and restaurants. On the southern slope of Mount Conero, beyond the ruins of a monastery, is the small medieval village of Sirolo. Perched on cliffs above a sheltered, pine-fringed bay, it welcomes visitors with its sinuous streets and, at its entrance, a pair of oaks reportedly planted by Saint Francis.

Travelers who venture inland from the seaside discover that the Marches loses none of its charm away from the clear blue waters. It claims two extraordinary Renaissance towns, Ascoli Piceno and Urbino, as well as the modern birthplace of paper making, Fabriano, which lies west of Ancona. The manufacture of paper here dates back to the late thirteenth century, when the first factory was opened, and today local residents continue to make their legendary product by both traditional and modern methods.

CALAMARI SOUP
ZUPETTA DI CALAMARI

SERVES FOUR

If you have already cleaned the squid, the soup is easily prepared just before serving. But you can also make in the morning or at midday and then reheat it very gently to serve at dinnertime.

Preparation:

1 First, clean the squid: Working with 1 squid at a time, cut off the tentacles just above the eyes. Squeeze the base of the tentacles to pop out the hard beak. Rinse the tentacles well and set aside whole. Pull out and discard the cartilage-like "quill" from the body, then rinse the body well, discarding the entrails. Carefully pull off the thin, mottled skin that covers the body, rinse the body again. If the squid bodies are not bite-size, cut them crosswise into $1/2$-inch pieces. Set them aside with the tentacles. Repeat with the remaining squid and pat dry.

2 In a saucepan over medium heat, warm the olive oil. Add the garlic and red onion and cook until softened, 2 to 3 minutes. Do not allow the garlic and onion to brown. Add the squid and cherry tomatoes and stir to combine. Pour in the hot stock and cook, stirring, until the squid is just done. They will curl up slightly and turn opaque. Do not overcook, as they will toughen. Season with salt and add the parsley.

3 Ladle into warmed bowls and garnish with the sprigs of basil, if desired. Serve at once.

1 POUND SMALL SQUID

2 TABLESPOONS EXTRA-VIRGIN OLIVE OIL

2 CLOVES GARLIC, CRUSHED

1 RED ONION, CUT INTO NARROW WEDGES

12 CHERRY TOMATOES, STEMMED AND HALVED

2 CUPS VEGETABLE STOCK (PAGE 158), HEATED

SALT

3 TABLESPOONS FRESH FLAT-LEAF PARSLEY

SMALL FRESH BASIL SPRIGS FOR GARNISH (OPTIONAL)

MUSSELS IN TOMATO SAUCE
COZZE ALLA MARINARA

The seaside towns and cities of the Marches boast a large repertory of seafood dishes, including fish chowder, *scapece* (pickled fish), squid in a wine sauce, and various grilled and roasted fish. Here, mussels are tossed in a quick tomato sauce seasoned with just a hint of chili.

2 TABLESPOONS EXTRA-VIRGIN OLIVE OIL

2 CLOVES GARLIC, CRUSHED

1 OR 2 SMALL DRIED CHILI PEPPERS

2 ¼ POUNDS MUSSELS, WELL SCRUBBED AND DEBEARDED

½ CUP DRY WHITE WINE

8 CHERRY TOMATOES, STEMMED AND CHOPPED

SALT

ABOUT 3 TABLESPOONS CHOPPED FRESH FLAT-LEAF PARSLEY

Preparation:

1 In a large saucepan with a tight-fitting lid, warm the olive oil over medium-high heat. Add the garlic and chili peppers and cook, stirring, until golden brown, about 3 minutes. Add the mussels, discarding any that do not close to the touch, along with the wine and tomatoes. Season lightly with salt and add 2 tablespoons of parsley. (It is important to season lightly, as the mussels may be salty from the sea.) Cover and cook, shaking the pan occasionally, until all the mussels open, 2 to 3 minutes. Do not overcook, or they will be rubbery. Discard any mussels that fail to open.

2 Ladle the mussels into a wide bowl and pour the cooking broth over the top. Sprinkle with the remaining 1 tablespoon of parsley and serve at once.

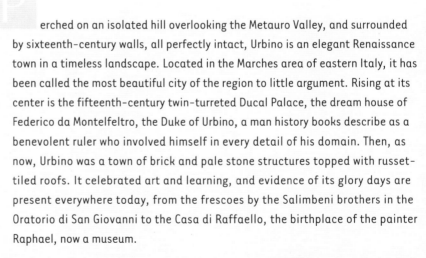

Urbino

Perched on an isolated hill overlooking the Metauro Valley, and surrounded by sixteenth-century walls, all perfectly intact, Urbino is an elegant Renaissance town in a timeless landscape. Located in the Marches area of eastern Italy, it has been called the most beautiful city of the region to little argument. Rising at its center is the fifteenth-century twin-turreted Ducal Palace, the dream house of Federico da Montelfeltro, the Duke of Urbino, a man history books describe as a benevolent ruler who involved himself in every detail of his domain. Then, as now, Urbino was a town of brick and pale stone structures topped with russet-tiled roofs. It celebrated art and learning, and evidence of its glory days are present everywhere today, from the frescoes by the Salimbeni brothers in the Oratorio di San Giovanni to the Casa di Raffaello, the birthplace of the painter Raphael, now a museum.

Urbino makes a comfortable base from which to visit a web of charming inland towns. Urbania, which lies to the southwest in the upper Metauro Valley, and has a smaller Ducal Palace, continues the tradition of hand-painted ceramics begun in the area in the Renaissance. The dukes of Urbino built a palace on a hilltop in the small, nearby town of Fossombrone as well. Gastronomes will head southwest from Fossombrone to Cagli, at the confluence of the Murano and Rosso Rivers, where both black and white truffles are found in the fall and wrought-iron pieces made by local craftsmen are available year-round.

PASTA IN A SACK WITH PORCINI CREAM
PASTA NEL SACCO CON CREMA DI PORCINI

SERVES FOUR

This is an old-fashioned country recipe that was traditionally made for special occasions. Fine pecorino cheeses are manufactured in the Marches, and black truffles are gathered in the hills near the border with Emilia-Romagna, as well as farther south, close to Umbria.

Preparation:

1 To make the pasta, whisk the eggs in a large bowl until the yolks and whites are well blended. Add the cheeses, nutmeg, salt and pepper to taste, lemon zest, and flour and beat well to combine. Add the melted butter and continue to beat for 15 minutes. This will release the gluten in the flour and the mixture will become a smooth paste similar in consistency to polenta.

2 Lay a clean cotton cloth about 2 feet square on a work surface. Pour the flour mixture into the center of the cloth. Fold the side of the cloth nearest you over the mixture and then fold the opposite side, shaping a log. Secure the ends by twisting closed and then tie tightly with kitchen twine.

3 In a large, wide saucepan, bring the vegetable stock to a boil. Carefully slip the "sack" into the stock, adjust the heat to a gentle simmer, and cook for 1 hour.

4 Remove the sack from the broth and let cool for 2 hours. Snip the strings and unwrap the pasta. Slice into 1/4-inch-thick rounds, and cut the rounds into 1/4-inch dice. Set aside.

5 To make the porcini cream, in a sauté pan over medium heat, melt the butter. Add the porcini, tomato, garlic, and parsley and raise the heat to high. Season with salt and pepper and cook, stirring, until the mushrooms are tender, 1 to 2 minutes.

6 Remove from the heat and transfer to a blender. Add 1 cup of the stock and purée until creamy. Return the mixture to the pan over medium-low heat, add the diced pasta and the remaining 1/2 cup stock and heat through gently, to allow the pasta to absorb the flavors of the sauce. As soon as the mixture begins to bubble, remove the pan from the heat.

7 Divide among warmed individual bowls and garnish with a little truffle, if desired. Serve immediately.

FOR THE PASTA:

5 EGGS

3/4 CUP PLUS 2 TABLESPOONS GRATED PARMIGIANO-REGGIANO CHEESE

1/4 CUP GRATED PECORINO CHEESE

SPRINKLING OF FRESHLY GRATED NUTMEG

SALT AND FRESHLY GROUND BLACK PEPPER

GRATED ZEST FROM 1/2 LEMON

3/4 CUP PLUS 2 TABLESPOONS SUPERFINE SOFT-WHEAT FLOUR SUCH AS CAKE FLOUR OR PASTRY FLOUR

7 TABLESPOONS UNSALTED BUTTER, MELTED AND COOLED

3 TO 4 QUARTS VEGETABLE STOCK (PAGE 158)

FOR THE PORCINI CREAM:

1 TABLESPOON UNSALTED BUTTER

3 1/2 OUNCES FRESH PORCINI, BRUSHED CLEAN AND THINLY SLICED

1 RIPE TOMATO, PEELED AND CRUSHED TO RELEASE EXCESS JUICE

1 CLOVE GARLIC, CRUSHED

2 TABLESPOONS CHOPPED FRESH FLAT-LEAF PARSLEY

SALT AND FRESHLY GROUND BLACK PEPPER

1 1/2 CUPS VEGETABLE STOCK (PAGE 158), HEATED

BLACK TRUFFLE SLIVERS (OPTIONAL)

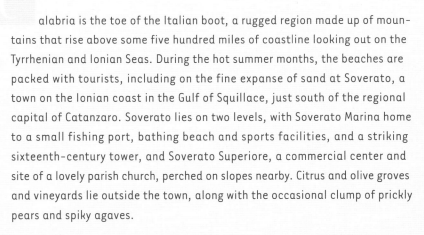

Soverato

alabria is the toe of the Italian boot, a rugged region made up of mountains that rise above some five hundred miles of coastline looking out on the Tyrrhenian and Ionian Seas. During the hot summer months, the beaches are packed with tourists, including on the fine expanse of sand at Soverato, a town on the Ionian coast in the Gulf of Squillace, just south of the regional capital of Catanzaro. Soverato lies on two levels, with Soverato Marina home to a small fishing port, bathing beach and sports facilities, and a striking sixteenth-century tower, and Soverato Superiore, a commercial center and site of a lovely parish church, perched on slopes nearby. Citrus and olive groves and vineyards lie outside the town, along with the occasional clump of prickly pears and spiky agaves.

South of Soverato, and away from the coast, lies the village of Stilo, situated halfway up the Stilaro Valley, against the rocky lower slopes of Mount Consolino. The town is much visited for its tenth-century Cattolica, one of the best-preserved Byzantine structures in the country. Other buildings—a medieval cathedral with a fine Gothic portal, the late-Renaissance church of San Giovanni, the ruins of an eleventh-century castle—draw travelers as well. Farther down the coast, the seaside town of Locri, an agricultural center known for its lamb and kid dishes and its local wines, has a museum of ancient Greek objects from a nearby excavation. Gerace, inland from Locri, is recognized for its production of pottery, hand-woven fabrics, and sheep's milk, ricotta-style cheeses.

The sea—both the Tyrrhenian and the Ionian—defines much of the Calabrian table, with tuna and swordfish the culinary royalty of the catch. But vegetables are important too: tossed with pasta, grilled and splashed with olive oil, baked with cheese, fried for fritters. Every meal, of course, is accompanied with wine, a very old custom, as the history of Calabrian viticulture reaches back to at least the sixth century B.C.

OCTOPUS WITH BROCCOLI AND MINT
POLIPO CON BROCCOLI E MENTA

SERVES FOUR

Simple yet satisfying, this typical Calabrian seaside dish goes together quickly once the octopus has been boiled. The addition of basil and mint near the end of cooking imparts a light, fresh taste to the finished dish.

Preparation:

1 Octopus is typically sold precleaned. If it has not been cleaned, invert it—much like you might turn a sock inside out—and remove the beak and viscera from the mouth, including the ink sac, rinsing well under running cold water. To tenderize it, bring a large pot of water to a boil and, holding the octopus by its mantle, dip it into the boiling water for about 10 seconds and pull it out. Let it cool slightly, then dip it again. Repeat 1 or 2 more times.

2 After the final dip, add the octopus to the boiling water and cook until tender, 1 to 1 $1/2$ hours. Drain the octopus, let cool, then cut the tentacles into $1/2$-inch-thick slices. Set aside.

3 Bring a saucepan of water to a boil. Add salt to taste and the broccoli and boil until just tender, about 5 minutes. Drain well and reserve.

4 In a sauté pan over medium-high heat, warm the olive oil. Add the garlic and sauté until lightly golden, about 2 minutes. Add the octopus, broccoli, basil, and mint and stir well to coat evenly with the oil and to heat through, just for a few minutes.

6 Season with salt and spoon into a warmed serving dish. Serve immediately.

1 LARGE OCTOPUS, ABOUT 2 POUNDS

SALT

4 BROCCOLI CROWNS, DIVIDED INTO FLORETS

4 TO 6 TABLESPOONS EXTRA-VIRGIN OLIVE OIL

1 CLOVE GARLIC, CHOPPED

5 FRESH BASIL LEAVES

5 FRESH MINT LEAVES

OVEN-BAKED FISH WITH VEGETABLES
PESCE AL FORNO

SERVES FOUR

Some of Calabria's finest ingredients are showcased in this recipe: fish from the local waters, vegetables from the region's carefully tended plots, and chestnuts from trees that dot the hillsides.

16 CHESTNUTS

1 CUP EXTRA-VIRGIN OLIVE OIL

1 CUP WATER

1 JOHN DORY, BLACK BASS, OR SALMON, ABOUT 4 POUNDS, CLEANED

SALT

2 CLOVES GARLIC, CRUSHED

10 FRESH BASIL LEAVES

4 FRESH FLAT-LEAF PARSLEY SPRIGS

2 POUNDS NEW POTATOES, HALVED

4 ZUCCHINI, QUARTERED LENGTHWISE

2 SMALL RED ONIONS, CUT INTO WEDGES

2 FRESH ROSEMARY SPRIGS

4 BAY LEAVES

Preparation:

1 In a saucepan, combine the chestnuts with water to cover. Bring to a boil and cook for 45 minutes. Drain and peel, removing the hard outer shell and the thin, furry skin beneath it. Reserve for garnish.

2 While the chestnuts are cooking, position a rack in the lower third of the oven and preheat to 500°F. Select a roasting pan that is large enough to hold the fish and still leave at least 4 inches on either side. Add the olive oil and then the water to the pan. Place the fish in the pan. Season the cavity of the fish with a little salt and the garlic, basil, and parsley. Scatter the potatoes around the fish and cover the potatoes with the zucchini and onions. Scatter the rosemary and bay leaves over the top and season the fish and vegetables with salt.

3 Place the pan in the oven and bake until the flesh of the fish flakes when pierced with a fork and the potatoes are tender, 35 to 40 minutes. Remove the fish from the oven. Break up 3 or 4 of the chestnuts and scatter the pieces and the remaining whole chestnuts over the fish.

4 To serve, bring the roasting pan to the table. Discard the bay leaves and whole herb sprigs. Divide the vegetables evenly among warmed individual plates. Starting at the back of the fish, lift away the flesh from the bones and place over the vegetables, again dividing evenly. Spoon some of the juices that accumulated in the pan over each portion, then serve immediately.

Maremma

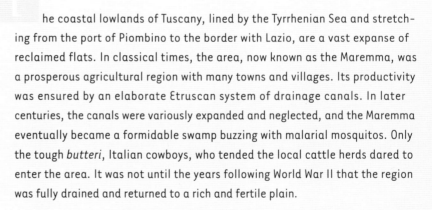

he coastal lowlands of Tuscany, lined by the Tyrrhenian Sea and stretching from the port of Piombino to the border with Lazio, are a vast expanse of reclaimed flats. In classical times, the area, now known as the Maremma, was a prosperous agricultural region with many towns and villages. Its productivity was ensured by an elaborate Etruscan system of drainage canals. In later centuries, the canals were variously expanded and neglected, and the Maremma eventually became a formidable swamp buzzing with malarial mosquitos. Only the tough *butteri*, Italian cowboys, who tended the local cattle herds dared to enter the area. It was not until the years following World War II that the region was fully drained and returned to a rich and fertile plain.

Today, two ancient and beautiful ports, Porto Ercole and Porto Santo Stefano, welcome a steady stream of sailboats to the Maremma coast. Both were founded by the Romans and both were sleepy fishing villages until vacationers discovered their charms. Porto Ercole, its harbor flanked by a pair of Spanish fortresses, is the smaller and more appealing of the two, with a graceful Gothic portal leading to its old center. Porto Santo Stefano, with a lively fish market and a sizable aggregation of hotels, was once an important port in the ancient world. Some of the vessels, alas, failed to navigate the harbor, and in recent years Phoenician amphorae and oil lamps have been pulled from the remains of sunken ships that litter the seabed not far from the shore.

The cooks of the Maremma combine the best from the sea and the land. Local waters deliver an abundance of sea bass, sardines, eels, and shellfish, while cattle, sheep, and goats are raised away from the coast. Game is much prized in the kitchen too, especially wild boar for simmering in sauces for *gnocchi* or *pappardelle*, braising with tomatoes, red wine, and herbs, or making into sausage laced with *peperoncino*.

SMOKED EEL
ANGUILLA AFFUMICATA

SERVES FOUR

The saltwater lagoons of the Maremma, near Orbetello, are home to a bounty of wiry eels. Although most Italians prefer to buy the eels live, much of the catch is sent to local smokehouses, where it is placed above smoldering fires scented with herbs. The smoked eels are usually briefly grilled or sautéed before serving.

Preparation:

1 In a sauté pan over medium-high heat, warm the olive oil.

2 Add the eels and sauté, tossing to coat with the oil, for 1 to 2 minutes.

3 Transfer to warmed individual plates and serve at once.

3 TABLESPOONS EXTRA-VIRGIN OLIVE OIL

4 SMOKED EELS, EACH CUT INTO PIECES 3 TO 4 INCHES LONG

"COOKED WATER"
ACQUACOTTA

SERVES FOUR

In the past, *acquacotta* was a humble soup, common fare for the cowherds and shepherds of the Maremma. For generations it was traditionally made from only water, bread, and herbs, and perhaps a bit of tomato, onion, or whatever was on hand, thus the name. Today, it is considerably more elaborate, and each town and village has its own version, but the name has remained in memory of past hard times.

1 BUNCH DANDELION GREENS, TRIMMED
AND COARSELY CHOPPED

1 BUNCH SWISS CHARD, TRIMMED AND
COARSELY CHOPPED

8 RIPE TOMATOES, PEELED AND SEEDED

3 YELLOW ONIONS, THINLY SLICED

4 CELERY STALKS, CHOPPED

6 FRESH BASIL LEAVES, CHOPPED

1 OR 2 SMALL DRIED CHILI PEPPERS, CRUSHED

SALT

6 CUPS WATER

½ CUP EXTRA-VIRGIN OLIVE OIL

4 EGGS

CROUTONS (PAGE 158)

3 TABLESPOONS GRATED
PARMIGIANO-REGGIANO CHEESE

Preparation:

1 In a large saucepan, combine the dandelion greens, Swiss chard, tomatoes, onions, celery, basil, and chili peppers. Stir to combine and break up the tomatoes. Season with salt. Add the water and drizzle the olive oil over all. Bring to a boil, reduce the heat to medium, cover partially, and simmer gently for 1 hour to develop a flavorful soup.

2 Taste and adjust the seasoning. Carefully break the eggs into the simmering soup and allow them to poach until the whites are set but the yolks are still liquid, about 2 minutes.

3 Place a few croutons in the bottom of each warmed soup bowl and sprinkle evenly with the cheese. Ladle in the hot soup, dividing the eggs evenly among the bowls. Serve at once.

Amalfi

The Amalfi coast, beginning south of Naples, just beyond Sorrento, and ending at the town of Salerno, has been called the single most spectacular swath of scenery in the Mediterranean. And it is indeed magnificent, with mountain after mountain rising straight from the sea. A threadlike corniche carries the traveler from the water's edge to hundreds of feet above it and down again in a series of tight twists and turns to daunt all but the most fearless driver. Rocky promontories alternate with lush valleys, and picturesque climbing villages trade views with hamlets crowded into coves. Most of the communities are a blinding Moorish white, but some are a pastiche of pale yellow, ivory, and dusty pink, and all of them are filled with flowers.

Positano, a picture-postcard vertical village that drew artists and writers before World War II and now attracts mostly the wealthy, is the best-known town along the route. But the smaller Amalfi has its own attractions, which begin at the main square. The lovely *duomo*, balanced atop a long flight of stairs, marries a mix of styles—Moorish, Gothic, Romanesque, Lombard, Baroque—in a single structure renowned all over Italy for its bronze doors cast in Constantinople in 1066. Garden lovers will want to stop at the mountain town of Ravello, a little farther down the coast and up a steep, winding road that discourages tour bus drivers. There, two villas, Cimbrone and Rufolo, each offer a paradise of flowers.

Locals insist that the lemons grown along the Amalfi coast are the tastiest in the world. They go into making one of the area's best-known products, *limoncello*, an intensely flavored liqueur that is drunk ice cold. Ideally, the lemons are peeled by hand and the rinds are then combined with only alcohol, water, and sugar to create the sunny yellow drink that is sipped either before or after dinner.

FESTIVAL PASTA
SCIALATIELLI

SERVES FOUR

The name for this short, narrow pasta, a favorite on the Amalfi coast, comes from the Neapolitan dialect word *sciarlare*, roughly "to have a fun time."

Preparation:

1 In a large bowl, combine the flour, parsley, cheese, and a sprinkling each of salt and pepper. Using your fingers, mix the ingredients together well. Add the egg, olive oil, and 1 cup of the milk, and mix with your hands to combine. Add more milk as needed to form a dough that holds together.

2 Turn out the dough onto a lightly floured work surface and knead until smooth and elastic, about 10 minutes. Cover with plastic wrap and let rest for 30 minutes.

3 Cut the dough into 3 equal portions. Clean the work surface as needed, then again dust with flour. Roll out each dough portion into a rectangle about 1/8 inch thick. Cut each rectangle into smaller rectangles about 6 inches long by 2 1/2 inches wide. Then cut each rectangle again into strips 2 1/2 inches long by 1/8 inch wide. Transfer to a baking sheet or similar pan and dust lightly with semolina flour to prevent sticking. (Use immediately, or wrap well and store in the freezer for up to 1 month.)

4 To cook the pasta, bring a large pot of water to a boil. Add salt to taste. Shake off the excess semolina flour from the pasta and add to the boiling water. Stir once and cook until almost *al dente*, 2 to 3 minutes. Drain and add to the sauce of choice. Follow the directions in the sauce recipes to complete the dish.

4 1/2 CUPS SUPERFINE SOFT-WHEAT FLOUR SUCH AS CAKE OR PASTRY FLOUR

1 TABLESPOON FINELY CHOPPED FRESH FLAT-LEAF PARSLEY

1/2 CUP GRATED PARMIGIANO-REGGIANO CHEESE

SALT AND FRESHLY GROUND BLACK PEPPER

1 EGG

1/2 CUP EXTRA-VIRGIN OLIVE OIL

1 TO 1 1/4 CUPS MILK

SEMOLINA FLOUR FOR DUSTING

TOMATO SAUCE WITH EGGPLANT AND MOZZARELLA (PAGE 124) OR FRUIT OF THE SEA SAUCE (PAGE 126)

TOMATO SAUCE WITH EGGPLANT AND MOZZARELLA

SALSA DI POMODORO CON MELANZANE E MOZZARELLA

SERVES FOUR

The Amalfi coast—indeed, the whole of Campania—is praised throughout Italy for its superb fruits and vegetables, but it is Amalfi's cheese that is world famous. Fresh *mozzarella di bufala*, made from the milk of water buffaloes descended from Indian stock, is distinguished by its slightly sour flavor and soft yet resilient texture. It is typically used atop pizzas or simply paired with the sun-ripened tomatoes and basil of the region.

1 EGGPLANT

SALT

7 TABLESPOONS EXTRA-VIRGIN OLIVE OIL

1 YELLOW ONION, CHOPPED

1 GENEROUS POUND RIPE TOMATOES, PEELED AND CRUSHED TO RELEASE EXCESS JUICE

SALT

4 FRESH BASIL LEAVES, CHOPPED

FESTIVAL PASTA (PAGE 123), COOKED UNTIL ALMOST AL DENTE AND DRAINED

1 TABLESPOON GRATED PARMIGIANO-REGGIANO CHEESE

1 TABLESPOON GRATED PECORINO CHEESE

7 OUNCES FRESH MOZZARELLA CHEESE, FINELY DICED

Preparation:

1 Trim the eggplant and then cut into $1/2$-inch cubes. Place in a colander, sprinkling each layer with salt, and place in the sink or over a bowl for about 15 minutes, to allow the bitter juices to drain off. Rinse briefly and pat dry.

2 In a sauté pan over high heat, warm 5 tablespoons of the olive oil. Working in batches if necessary, fry the eggplant until browned and tender, 5 to 10 minutes. Drain off any excess oil and set aside.

3 In another sauté pan over medium-high heat, warm the remaining 2 tablespoons of olive oil. Add the onion and sauté until softened, 2 to 3 minutes. Add the tomatoes, season with salt, and add half of the basil. Simmer for 2 to 3 minutes to blend the flavors.

4 Add the reserved eggplant and the pasta and toss to combine. Add the 3 cheeses and the remaining basil and cook briefly until the cheese has melted and the pasta is *al dente* and has absorbed a little of the sauce.

5 Transfer to a warm serving bowl or individual plates and serve at once.

FRUIT OF THE SEA SAUCE
SALSA AL FRUTTI DI MARE

Cherry tomatoes often carry the most intense tomato flavor, making them excellent for use in this rustic sauce. Once the shellfish have been scrubbed, the sauce goes together quickly. Be sure not to cook the clams and mussels too long, or they will toughen.

2 POUNDS MIXED CLAMS AND MUSSELS

SALT

7 TABLESPOONS EXTRA-VIRGIN OLIVE OIL

2 CLOVES GARLIC, CHOPPED

2 TABLESPOONS CHOPPED FRESH
FLAT-LEAF PARSLEY

FRESHLY GROUND BLACK PEPPER

10 CHERRY TOMATOES, STEMMED AND CHOPPED

FESTIVAL PASTA (PAGE 123), COOKED UNTIL
ALMOST *AL DENTE* AND DRAINED

Preparation:

1 Scrub the clams and mussels well, discarding those that do not close to the touch. Debeard the mussels. Place the clams in a large bowl filled with salted water and let stand for about 15 minutes. (This encourages them to expel any sand.) Drain and set aside with the mussels.

2 In a large sauté pan over medium-high heat, warm the olive oil. Add the garlic and parsley and sauté until the garlic is lightly golden, 2 to 3 minutes. Add the clams and mussels, cover, and cook, shaking the pan occasionally, until the shellfish open, 2 to 3 minutes. Uncover, season with salt and pepper, add the tomatoes, and heat through. Discard any clams or mussels that fail to open.

3 Add the pasta to the pan, toss to combine, and cook, stirring until the pasta is *al dente* and has absorbed a little of the sauce.

4 Transfer to a warmed serving bowl or individual plates and serve immediately.

Pozzuoli

Only ten miles west of sprawling Naples, Pozzuoli is today little more than a suburb, but in the time of Julius Caesar, it enjoyed great prosperity and was the largest trading port in the western Mediterranean. Traces of the old port remain alongside the city's contemporary jetties.

A Roman marketplace once occupied a porticoed grand square on what is now via Roma. Its ruins reveal that the main hall included a dome-covered fountain and was rimmed with stalls that faced the courtyard and the sea beyond. Evidence of the market was lost for centuries, only to reappear following volcanic activity in the sixteenth century. Nearby are the well-preserved ruins of a first-century amphitheater, the third largest in Italy. It held over forty thousand spectators, all of whom came to cheer on wild-beast fights, mock sea battles, and the occasional Christian martyrdom.

Volcanoes dot the area around Pozzuoli, and travelers interested in seeing one close up can stop at the inactive Solfatara, a sunken crater some twenty-five hundred feet in diameter. Beneath the ground, the temperature rises to about 800 degrees Fahrenheit, producing fumaroles (jets of sulfurous smoke) that curl upward through the crater's cracks. According to local legend, the smoky discharges are the poisons that flowed from the wounds the Titans sustained in their war with Zeus, before he dispatched them to Hades, the Greek Hell.

The rich volcanic soil and sunny climate of Campania fill local market bins with an extraordinary array of vegetables, fruits, and nuts: tomatoes, zucchini, eggplants, olives, lemons, oranges, figs, melons, pomegranates, walnuts, and almonds. Nearby vendors and shops display *salame napoletano* and other fresh and cured sausages; cheeses such as mozzarella, caciocavallo, and scamorza; and other irresistible local products, including the best-known white wine of the region, Lacryma Cristi (Tears of Christ).

BAKED MUSSELS WITH BREAD CRUMBS
COZZE GRATINATE

SERVES FOUR

Mussels are popular in Naples and surrounding communities, where they are served in a peppery wine broth, tossed with pasta, combined with other shellfish in a seafood salad, or baked, as they are here, with a crusty bread crumb topping.

Preparation:

1 Preheat the oven to 350°F.

2 Scrub the mussels well, discarding those that do not close to the touch, then debeard them. Working with 1 mussel at a time and positioning it over a bowl to catch the juices, gently twist the shells to open slightly. Slide a paring knife between the 2 shells, and run the knife between the mussel and the top shell to free the meat. Discard the top shell. Run the knife along the bottom shell to free the meat, but leave the meat in the shell. Place the mussel on the half shell in a shallow pan. Repeat until all the mussels are opened and arranged in a single layer in the pan.

3 Spoon some of the captured juices over each mussel. Top each with a small knob of butter. Drizzle the olive oil evenly over all. Sprinkle bread crumbs over each mussel to cover completely.

4 Place in the oven and bake until the crumbs form a golden brown crust, about 10 minutes. Transfer to a serving platter or divide among individual plates and serve either hot or at room temperature.

2 POUNDS MUSSELS

1/2 CUP PLUS 2 TABLESPOONS UNSALTED BUTTER

2 TABLESPOONS EXTRA-VIRGIN OLIVE OIL

1 3/4 CUPS FIND DRIED BREAD CRUMBS, PREFERABLY HOMEMADE

PASTA WITH BEANS AND MUSSELS
PASTA E FAGIOLI CON COZZE

Regional versions of *pasta e fagioli*, usually a thick soup of pasta and beans, are eaten in Trentino, Veneto, Sicily, and elsewhere in Italy. This recipe includes mussels to satisfy the seafood lovers of Campania.

2 CUPS DRIED WHITE BEANS

2 POUNDS MUSSELS

2 TABLESPOONS EXTRA-VIRGIN OLIVE OIL

10 OUNCES PROSCIUTTO, CUT INTO SMALL PIECES

1 YELLOW ONION, FINELY CHOPPED

2 CELERY STALKS, CHOPPED

5 CLOVES GARLIC, CRUSHED

1/2 FRESH RED CHILI PEPPER, CHOPPED

6 TO 8 CHERRY TOMATOES, STEMMED AND HALVED

6 CUPS WATER

14 OUNCES DRIED TUBETTI PASTA

SALT

Preparation:

1 Pick over the beans and rinse well. Place in a bowl with water to cover and let stand overnight. The next day, drain, place in a saucepan, and add water to cover. Bring to a boil, reduce the heat to medium, cover partially, and cook until almost tender, about 45 minutes. Drain and reserve.

2 Scrub the mussels well, discarding those that do not close to the touch, then debeard them.

3 In a saucepan over medium heat, warm the olive oil. Add the prosciutto, onion, celery, garlic, chili pepper, and tomatoes. Cook, stirring, until the vegetables soften, about 5 minutes. Do not allow them to brown.

4 Add the drained beans and continue to cook, stirring for about 10 minutes to blend all the ingredients fully. Pour in the water, raise the heat to high, and bring to a boil. Add the mussels and the pasta and cook, stirring occasionally, until the pasta is *al dente*, and the mussels have opened, 10 to 12 minutes longer. Taste and adjust the seasoning with salt. (It may not need any, as the mussels and their juices will be salty from the sea and the prosciutto is salty as well.)

5 Ladle into warmed soup plates and serve immediately.

Gaeta

earby orange trees, olive groves, and vineyards and its position on a sandy headland facing the sea give the town of Gaeta a thoroughly Mediterranean setting. Known for its rich archaeological finds, panoramic views, swimming beaches, and good food, this medieval walled town is located about halfway between Rome and Naples near Lazio's southern border and is a favorite summer getaway for Italians looking to escape the heat and pressures of urban life. They stroll the narrow streets, visit the small museum housing second-century sculptures excavated from local sites, sun themselves on the sandy beaches, and fill the waterfront seafood restaurants, where the wines of neighboring Campania are generously poured.

Gaeta's still-visible walls and ramparts served to protect the northern border of the Bourbon-ruled Kingdom of Naples, while later they did the same for the Kingdom of Two Sicilies, which disappeared with the unification of Italy in 1861. But the ruins of Roman villas, including the villa and grotto of the notoriously hedonistic Emperor Tiberius, prove that Gaeta was an important player long before the days of the Bourbons. So, too, does the tomb of Cicero, ancient Rome's most famous senator. A stately sepulchre on a square base, it lies not far from the crossroads of the famed Appian Way and of the small, beautiful resort and port of Sperlonga, a medieval settlement that mimics the shape of a Roman amphitheater. The town sits high on a cliff overlooking the Tyrrhenian Sea, with sandy beaches stretching out below it on either side.

Outside of Italy, Gaeta is perhaps most closely linked with the black olives of the same name. Two types are produced here: small, purplish black olives preserved in brine, and larger, meatier olives dry-salt cured and then coated with olive oil. In the port of Gaeta, seaside restaurants offer the local mussels in soup and tossed with pastas and concoct ever-changing *fritti misti di mare* based on the catch of the day.

RISOTTO WITH SHRIMP AND ZUCCHINI
RISOTTO CON GAMBERETTI E ZUCCHINI

SERVES FOUR

Italian cooks all along the boot regularly combine seafood—mussels, clams, eel, lobster, sole, bass—and the plump, short-grained rice of the north's Po Valley to create the risottos that are among the best-known dishes of the country. The Gulf of Gaeta has long been a source of shrimp, which are used in the local risotto.

Preparation:

1 Pour the water into a saucepan and bring to a boil. Adjust the heat to keep the water hot. In a heavy saucepan over medium-high heat, warm the olive oil. Add the garlic and zucchini and sauté until softened, about 2 minutes. Add the rice and stir until the grains are well coated with the oil and and opaque, 3 to 4 minutes. Add the wine and stir until nearly absorbed. Add the tomato and one-half of the parsley and stir to combine. Season with salt.

2 Add a ladleful (about 1 cup) of the water, adjust the heat to maintain a gentle simmer, and cook, stirring continuously, until the water is absorbed, 2 to 3 minutes. Continue adding the water, a ladleful at a time and stirring continuously, for 10 minutes. Add the cream and stir until absorbed, then add more water and stir for 3 to 4 minutes. Add the shrimp and more water and stir for about 4 minutes. At this point, after a total cooking time of 18 to 20 minutes, the rice should be creamy, moist, and just tender but still slightly firm in the center. You may not need to add all of the water. Add the butter and stir to combine.

3 Taste and adjust the seasoning. Spoon onto warmed individual plates and sprinkle with the remaining parsley. Serve immediately.

6 CUPS WATER

7 TABLESPOONS EXTRA-VIRGIN OLIVE OIL

2 CLOVES GARLIC, CHOPPED

2 ZUCCHINI, TRIMMED AND JULIENNED

2 CUPS ARBORIO RICE

3/4 CUP DRY WHITE WINE

1 RIPE TOMATO, CHOPPED

1 CUP CHOPPED FRESH FLAT-LEAF PARSLEY

SALT

1 CUP HEAVY CREAM

14 OUNCES SMALL SHRIMP, PEELED AND DEVEINED

1/4 CUP UNSALTED BUTTER

BAKED SWORDFISH WITH BREAD CRUMBS
PESCE SPADA GRATINATO

SERVES FOUR

Much of Italy's culinary appeal derives from its long and varied coastline, and swordfish is a coveted catch from Lazio to Sicily. The meaty flesh is variously cured and served as an antipasto, thinly sliced and sautéed with tomatoes, or baked with a crusty topping of seasoned bread crumbs, as it is here.

$1/2$ CUP EXTRA-VIRGIN OLIVE OIL

4 SWORDFISH STEAKS

$1 3/4$ CUPS FINE DRIED BREAD CRUMBS, PREFERABLY FRESHLY MADE

1 CUP CHOPPED FRESH FLAT-LEAF PARSLEY

2 CLOVES GARLIC, CHOPPED

SALT AND FRESHLY GROUND BLACK PEPPER

Preparation:

1 Preheat the oven to 350°F.

2 Drizzle about one-fourth of the olive oil over the bottom of a shallow baking pan large enough to hold the swordfish steaks in a single layer. Place the steaks in the pan. In a bowl, stir together the bread crumbs, parsley, and garlic and season with salt and pepper. Distribute the bread crumbs evenly over the steaks. Drizzle the remaining $3/4$ cup olive oil over all.

3 Place in the oven and bake until the swordfish is just opaque throughout when pierced with a knife, about 10 minutes.

4 Remove from the oven, transfer to warmed individual plates, and serve immediately.

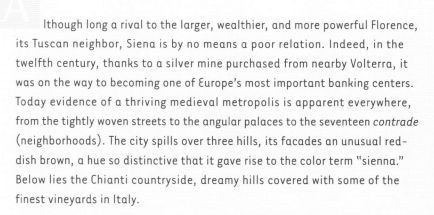

Siena

Siena

Although long a rival to the larger, wealthier, and more powerful Florence, its Tuscan neighbor, Siena is by no means a poor relation. Indeed, in the twelfth century, thanks to a silver mine purchased from nearby Volterra, it was on the way to becoming one of Europe's most important banking centers. Today evidence of a thriving medieval metropolis is apparent everywhere, from the tightly woven streets to the angular palaces to the seventeen *contrade* (neighborhoods). The city spills over three hills, its facades an unusual reddish brown, a hue so distinctive that it gave rise to the color term "sienna." Below lies the Chianti countryside, dreamy hills covered with some of the finest vineyards in Italy.

Siena is a treasure box of art and architecture, from its resplendent *duomo* to its imposing Piccolomini Palace to its countless loggias. But the heart of the city is the Campo, a fan-shaped *piazza* considered by most observers to be the loveliest in Tuscany. Its focal point is the Torre di Mangia, a needlelike tower topped by a bell that can be heard in every corner of the city and beyond. Twice a year, thousands of people come to this brick-paved square to watch the *Palio*, a horse race that, according to records, dates back to at least the thirteenth century. A dazzling pageant precedes the competition, then riders from each *contrada* compete to take home a special banner—a *palio*—to their neighborhood. Not surprisingly, come nightfall, the winning *contrada* is a swirl of Siennese, and visiting, party-goers.

Siena's most important contribution to the menu of Tuscan dishes is its sweets, many of them linked to religious celebrations but now made year-round. Almonds, walnuts, honey, candied fruits, and spices are common ingredients. *Panforte*—"strong bread"—is the star of the group, a rich, dense, flat Christmas fruitcake that reaches back to medieval times. Other specialties include *ricciarelli*, small, soft almond cookies, and *cavallucci*, highly seasoned spice cookies.

SLOW-COOKED VEAL IN CHIANTI WINE
STRACOTTO AL CHIANTI

SERVES FOUR

The secret to this stew is long, slow cooking and a good-quality Chianti made and bottled in the area that lies between Florence and Siena. Open a second bottle to serve along with the dish.

Preparation:

1 Layer the onion slices in the bottom of a wide, heavy pot. Arrange the veal pieces on top and season with salt and pepper. Drizzle the olive oil over all and stir to combine.

2 Place the pot over high heat and cook, stirring until the onions release their juices into the veal. Continue stirring over high heat until the veal begins to brown on all sides, 10 to 15 minutes. Pour in the wine and bring to a boil. Reduce the heat to low, cover partially, and cook until the meat is very tender, 2 1/2 to 3 hours. The meat will have absorbed most of the wine and the remainder will have reduced to a sauce consistency.

3 Transfer to a serving dish and serve hot or at warm room temperature.

2 POUNDS RED ONIONS, SLICED

2 POUNDS STEWING VEAL, CUT INTO 2-INCH CUBES

SALT AND FRESHLY GROUND BLACK PEPPER

1/2 CUP EXTRA-VIRGIN OLIVE OIL

1 BOTTLE (750 ML) FULL-BODIED RED CHIANTI WINE

COOKED CREAM WITH CHOCOLATE SAUCE
PANNA COTTA AL CIOCCOLATO

Cooked cream is a traditional Tuscan dish that has gained favor elsewhere in Italy. Here it is treated to a chocolate sauce, but other variations—caramel sauce, a scattering of fresh berries—are also popular. In Italy, leaf gelatin is used to set the cream, but it is difficult to find in the United States. The more widely available powdered gelatin is successfully substituted.

4 CUPS HEAVY CREAM

4 ENVELOPES UNFLAVORED POWDERED GELATIN

1/4 CUP CONFECTIONERS' SUGAR

4 SQUARES (1 OUNCE EACH) BITTERSWEET CHOCOLATE, CHOPPED

2 CUPS MILK

Preparation:

1 Pour 1/2 cup of the cream into a small saucepan, sprinkle the gelatin over the cream, let stand to soften, then dissolve over low heat, about 3 minutes. Meanwhile, place the remaining 3 1/2 cups cream and the sugar in a saucepan and place over medium heat. Bring to a boil, stirring to dissolve the sugar. Remove from the heat and stir in the gelatin mixture. Divide among individual serving bowls, cover, and refrigerate until set, at least 3 hours.

2 When ready to serve, combine the chocolate and milk in a heavy saucepan. Place over medium heat and stir until the chocolate is fully melted and a smooth sauce has formed. Remove from the heat.

3 Pour the warm sauce over the chilled *panna cotta*, dividing evenly. Serve immediately.

Orvieto

he people of Orvieto, less than two hours north of Rome by train, are quick to boast about their extraordinary views of the countryside. They owe this fine panorama to a now-extinct volcano, which long ago left behind the high tufa pedestal upon which the town stands. A natural stronghold since Etruscan times, Orvieto proved a safe haven during the Middle Ages for Popes who needed to flee Rome when their rulings were out of favor. The same volcano delivered a wealth of minerals to the land below, now covered with vineyards.

The town's most memorable structure is unquestionably the *duomo*, begun in 1290, with its triptych-like facade done in a rich palette of mosaics. The interior, with works by Luca Signorelli and Fra Angelico, is a treasure trove of fifteenth- and sixteenth-century Italian art, with images of such well-known figures as Christopher Columbus, Dante, and Petrarch pictured in one of the most celebrated fresco cycles of the Renaissance.

Beyond the Piazza del Duomo, the streets of Orvieto wind past a number of more modest churches, some sixteenth-century *palazzi*, neighborhoods of medieval houses, many artisan shops—primarily woodworkers but also lace makers—and what seems like an equal number of wine shops. The latter, of course, all stock the region's straw-colored wines, which are prized throughout the country and abroad.

Without question, Orvieto's greatest contribution to the table is its wine, a pleasant white with a pale yellow cast. Most Orvieto whites are dry, although a sweeter version, called Orvieto Abbocato, is also made and is wonderful at meal's end. Indeed, it was this sweet wine, the only type made during the Renaissance, that Luca Signorelli insisted be part of the payment for his fresco cycle in the *duomo*.

BEAN SOUP
ZUPPA DI FAGIOLI

SERVES FOUR

If you lack the time to soak the beans overnight, you can use the quick-soak method: Combine the rinsed beans with water to cover, bring just to a boil, cover, remove from the heat, and let stand for about 1 hour. Drain the beans and proceed as directed.

Preparation:

1 Pick over the beans and rinse well. Place in a bowl with water to cover and let stand overnight. The next day, drain and set aside.

2 Tie together the thyme, rosemary, sage, marjoram, and bay to make a bouquet garni. In a large, heavy-bottomed pan over medium-high heat, warm the 2 tablespoons of olive oil. Add the onions, carrot, and celery and sauté, stirring until the onions are lightly golden, about 5 minutes. Add the *bouquet garni*, drained beans, uncooked piece of bacon, garlic, and hot stock and bring to a boil. Cover, reduce the heat to low, and simmer until the beans are tender, 40 to 45 minutes.

3 Remove the bacon, garlic, and herb bundle and discard. Season the soup with salt and pepper. Let cool slightly, then transfer one-third of the beans to a blender and purée, leaving a little texture. Return the puree to the pan and reheat gently for about 10 minutes to achieve a good consistency.

4 Ladle the soup into bowls and crumble some of the fried bacon over each serving. Sprinkle with the cheese and drizzle with a little olive oil. Serve at once.

2 CUPS DRIED WHITE BEANS

1 OR 2 FRESH THYME SPRIGS

1 OR 2 FRESH ROSEMARY SPRIGS

1 OR 2 FRESH SAGE LEAVES

1 OR 2 FRESH MARJORAM SPRIGS

1 OR 2 BAY LEAVES

2 TABLESPOONS EXTRA-VIRGIN OLIVE OIL, PLUS OIL FOR DRIZZLING

1 YELLOW ONION, CHOPPED

1 CARROT, PEELED AND CHOPPED

1 CELERY STALK, CHOPPED

3 1/2 OUNCES UNCOOKED BACON, IN ONE PIECE

1 CLOVE GARLIC, CRUSHED

4 1/2 CUPS BEEF STOCK (PAGE 159) OR VEGETABLE STOCK (PAGE 158), HEATED

SALT AND FRESHLY GROUND BLACK PEPPER

2 OUNCES SLICED BACON, FRIED UNTIL CRISP

2 TABLESPOONS GRATED PARMIGIANO-REGGIANO CHEESE

DUCK BREAST WITH BLACK TRUFFLE SAUCE
PETTI D'ANITRA CON SALSA DI TARTUFO

SERVES FOUR

Be careful not to overcook the duck breasts. They should remain a bit red at the center for the best flavor and texture. If you are fortunate enough to come upon freshly dug truffles, rinse them briefly under cool water, then scrub gently with a small brush to remove any soil or other debris from the crevices. For grating, use the large holes of a handheld grater.

4 DUCK BREAST HALVES WITH SKIN INTACT

SALT AND FRESHLY GROUND BLACK PEPPER

7 TABLESPOONS UNSALTED BUTTER

1 TO 2 TABLESPOONS GRATED BLACK TRUFFLE

1 CUP VEGETABLE STOCK (PAGE 158)

2 TABLESPOONS THINLY SLICED BLACK TRUFFLE

Preparation:

1 Preheat the oven to 400°F.

2 Season the duck breasts on both sides with salt and pepper. Place a large sauté pan over high heat. When it is hot, add the duck breasts, skin side down. Transfer the pan to the oven and cook for about 10 minutes. Flip the breasts over and cook until medium-rare, about 5 minutes longer. Remove from the oven and transfer to a platter; keep warm while making the sauce.

3 Pour off the duck fat from the pan and return the pan to high heat. Add the butter, grated truffle, and stock and bring to a boil. Reduce to a slightly syrupy consistency. Season with salt and pepper and keep warm.

4 Cut each duck breast on the bias into 5 or 6 slices. Arrange the breasts on warmed individual plates and drizzle the sauce over each portion. Scatter the truffle slices over all and serve immediately.

Viterbo

Although today Viterbo is rather unassuming, it has had its moments of glory. Located in northern Lazio, it became the seat of the Popes in the thirteenth century, denying Rome, some fifty miles to the south, that honor. The decidedly squarish Papal Palace, with its Gothic loggia and classic crenellation, still stands in the Piazza San Lorenzo, flanked by a severe Romanesque church and the fifteenth-century Palazzo Farnese.

A walk along the via San Pellegrino brings you into Viterbo's oldest quarter, a plait of narrow streets and twisting alleys, towers and arcades, twin-windowed facades and exterior staircases. At its heart is the Piazza San Pellegrino, arguably the most picturesque spot in the town for its medieval ambience. Early each September, a torchlight procession is held during which a towering imitation belfry topped by the image of Santa Rosa, the patron saint of the town, is carried through the streets. But because this is Italy, the solemn religious ceremony is inevitably followed by much food, drink, and frivolity.

Outside Viterbo, to the east, is Villa Lante, with a particularly lovely Renaissance garden designed by Iacopo da Vignola in the late sixteenth century. To the west are thermal springs once enjoyed by the Etruscans and ancient Romans and now frequented by contemporary Italians.

Away from the sprawl of Rome, Lazio offers some welcome pockets of agriculture. In the Castelli Romani, southeast of the capital, grapes are grown for making the well-known Frascati wine. Pecorino romano and ricotta romana are also still produced in the region, although in smaller amounts than in the past, and the peas, artichokes, and spinach of Lazio continue to be prized—and anxiously awaited each season—by the locals.

CHESTNUT SOUP
ZUPPA DI CASTAGNE

SERVES FOUR

When the weather in Lazio turns cool in late fall, this soup goes onto stoves throughout the region. If possible, use canned Italian tomatoes, preferably the meaty, flavorful variety known as San Marzano, which are shaped like a flask when fresh and originated in a village near Pompeii. Cirio and La Valle are among the best brands.

Preparation:

1 Preheat the oven to 375°F.

2 Using a sharp paring knife, peel away the tough hard shell from each chestnut, which will reveal a furry undercoating. Place the chestnuts in a single layer in a roasting plan, place the pan in the oven, and roast for 10 minutes. Remove from the oven and, working with 1 chestnut at a time, scrape off the furry layer of skin. Act quickly, as it is easier to peel them while they are still warm. Set the nuts aside.

3 In a heavy-bottomed saucepan over medium-high heat, warm the olive oil. Add the garlic and sauté until lightly browned, 3 to 4 minutes. Add the tomato purée, stock, chestnuts, and salt, black pepper, and red pepper to taste. Cover, reduce the heat to low, and simmer until the chestnuts are tender, about 30 minutes. Taste and adjust the seasoning.

4 Divide the croutons among 4 warmed soup bowls. Ladle the soup over the top. Serve immediately.

2 POUNDS CHESTNUTS

1/3 CUP EXTRA-VIRGIN OLIVE OIL

2 CLOVES GARLIC, CHOPPED

1 1/2 CUPS PURÉED CANNED PLUM TOMATOES, PREFERABLY SAN MARZANO VARIETY

4 1/2 CUPS VEGETABLE STOCK (PAGE 158)

SALT, FRESHLY GROUND BLACK PEPPER, AND RED PEPPER FLAKES

1/2 CUP CROUTONS (PAGE 158)

ROLLED VEAL STUFFED WITH CHESTNUTS
VITELLO RIPIENO CON CASTAGNE

SERVES FOUR

Liguria claims the most celebrated recipe for stuffed breast of veal, with a filling of veal, sweetbreads, pistachios, herbs, cheese, and hard-boiled eggs. In Lazio, cooks stuff the meat with a filling based on chestnuts, which have been grown in the region for centuries.

1 POUND CHESTNUTS

1 BONELESS BREAST OF VEAL, ABOUT 2 POUNDS

SALT AND FRESHLY GROUND BLACK PEPPER

5 OR 6 SLICES PROSCIUTTO

1 EGG

2 TABLESPOONS FINE DRIED BREAD CRUMBS

ABOUT 3 TABLESPOONS EXTRA-VIRGIN OLIVE OIL

1 CLOVE GARLIC, QUARTERED LENGTHWISE

1 FRESH ROSEMARY SPRIG, BROKEN INTO PIECES

1 CUP DRY WHITE WINE

Preparation:

1 Using a paring knife, cut an X in the flat side of each chestnut. Place the chestnuts in a saucepan, add water to cover, bring to a boil, and cook for 35 minutes. Drain, rinse under cold water, and peel away the hard outer shell and thin, furry skin beneath it. Set aside.

2 Preheat the oven to 500°F.

3 Lay the veal breast on a work surface and season with salt and pepper. (Use salt sparingly, as prosciutto can be salty.) Lay the prosciutto slices over the veal in a single layer. In a bowl, beat the egg until blended and season with salt and pepper. Add the chestnuts and bread crumbs and stir to combine. Place the mixture in the center of the veal breast, roll up the veal into a cylinder, and tie securely, including the ends, with kitchen string to hold the stuffing in place.

4 Pour about 1 tablespoon of the olive oil into the bottom of a shallow roasting pan. Put the veal in the pan and season with salt and pepper. Place the garlic and rosemary pieces along the top of the veal roll and then drizzle the remaining olive oil over the top.

5 Place in the oven and roast for 1 hour. Remove the pan from the oven and pour the wine over the veal. Cover the pan tightly with aluminum foil, return to the oven, and cook until the meat is very tender when pierced with a knife, 10 to 15 minutes longer. Remove from the oven and transfer the veal roll to a platter. Let rest in a warm place for 15 to 20 minutes.

6 Skim off the fat from the pan juices and discard. Reheat the juices. Cut the veal roll into slices $1/2$ inch thick. Spoon the pan juices over the top and serve.

BASIC RECIPES

CROUTONS

MAKES 2 CUPS

Select a coarse country bread for making the croutons, and be sure to trim away the crusts before you cube the bread. This is a good way to use up day-old bread.

1/2 CUP EXTRA-VIRGIN OLIVE OIL

2 OR 3 CLOVES GARLIC, CRUSHED

2 CUPS CUBED BREAD (3/4-INCH CUBES AND WITHOUT CRUSTS)

Preparation:

1 In a large sauté pan over medium-high heat, warm the olive oil. Add the garlic cloves and sauté until golden brown, 3 to 4 minutes. Remove and discard the garlic. Raise the heat to high, add the bread cubes, and sauté, tossing often, until golden on all sides, about 5 minutes. Using a slotted spoon, transfer to paper towels to drain.

VEGETABLE STOCK

MAKES ABOUT 3 QUARTS

Other vegetables can be used for flavoring this stock, such as parsnips and bell peppers. Avoid strongly flavored or leafy green vegetables such as broccoli or spinach, however, as they will deliver an unappetizing taste and color. You may add other herbs, too, including marjoram, oregano, or thyme. Do not salt the stock. Instead, rely on the seasoning in the recipe in which it is used.

1 LARGE YELLOW ONION, CHOPPED

3 OR 4 CELERY STALKS, CHOPPED

2 OR 3 CARROTS, CHOPPED

1 LARGE LEEK, INCLUDING GREEN TOPS, CLEANED AND CHOPPED

1/4 POUND FRESH CULTIVATED WHITE AND/OR BROWN MUSHROOMS, BRUSHED CLEAN AND CHOPPED

1 LARGE OR 2 MEDIUM TOMATOES, CHOPPED

4 TO 6 CLOVES GARLIC, CRUSHED

1 BAY LEAF

6 BLACK PEPPERCORNS

STEMS FROM A HANDFUL OF FRESH FLAT-LEAF PARSLEY SPRIGS

Preparation:

1 Combine all the ingredients in a 3- to 5-quart saucepan and add water to cover by about 3 inches. Bring to a boil, reduce the heat to medium-low, and simmer, uncovered, for 1 hour.

2 Strain through a fine-mesh sieve and use as directed in individual recipes. The stock can be covered and refrigerated for up to 5 days or frozen for up to 6 months.

BEEF STOCK

MAKES ABOUT 3 QUARTS

You can double the ingredients to make a large batch of stock, and then store it in the freezer for up to 6 months. As with the vegetable stock, do not salt the stock; instead, rely on the seasoning of the dish in which it is used.

2 POUNDS BEEF SHANKS AND TRIMMINGS

2 SMALL CARROTS, PEELED AND CUT INTO 2-INCH PIECES

1 LARGE YELLOW ONION, CUT INTO 2-INCH PIECES

1 CELERY STALK, CUT INTO 2-INCH PIECES

$^1/_4$ CUP VEGETABLE OIL

$^1/_4$ POUND FRESH CULTIVATED WHITE AND/OR BROWN MUSHROOMS (OR MUSHROOM TRIMMINGS), BRUSHED CLEANED AND CHOPPED

1 TOMATO, DICED

1 BAY LEAF

5 OR 6 BLACK PEPPERCORNS

2 FRESH THYME SPRIGS

Preparation:

1 Preheat the oven to 400°F.

2 In a large, shallow roasting pan, combine the beef bones and trimmings, carrots, onion, and celery. Drizzle with the oil and turn the meat and vegetables to coat evenly. Roast until well browned, 45 to 50 minutes.

3 Remove the pan from the oven and transfer the beef and vegetables to a stock-pot, discarding any fat in the pan. Add cold water to cover along with the mushrooms, tomato, bay leaf, peppercorns, and thyme. Bring to a boil over high heat, skimming off any scum that rises to the surface. Reduce the heat to low and simmer, uncovered, for 2 to 3 hours, skimming occasionally to remove any fat or scum from the surface.

4 Remove from the heat and take out the solids with a large slotted spoon or a skimmer. Strain through a fine-mesh sieve, then cover and refrigerate for up to 5 days. Before using, lift off and discard the layer of fat that solidifies on the surface.

INDEX

TRIBUTE

FIRST AND FOREMOST—I would like to thank David and Nina Rocco for their enthusiasm and vision.

Producing a television series is truly a collaborative effort. We are grateful to our production team: Creator and Host, David Rocco; Producer and Director, Jim McKenna; Creator and Co-Producer, Nina Rocco; Executive in Charge of Production, Keith R. Buck; Director of Photography, Damir Chytil; Sound Recordist, Edward Krupa; Production Coordinator, Vittorio Pasquale; Editor, Mary Dorich; and Writer, Anne Hainsworth.

We would like to thank the Italian Government Travel Office and the regional tourism agencies of Italy, and dedicate this book to the many chefs and restaurants that provided our inspiration.

Thanks to television stations worldwide for broadcasting *Avventura, Journeys in Italian Cuisine*.

Thank you,

Charles Falzon, Executive Producer

Avventura, Journeys in Italian Cuisine is a presentation of American Public Television in the United States. Thank you to The Olive Garden for their sponsorship of the television series as seen on American Public Television.